THE TRUE BELIEVER

Thoughts on the Nature of Mass Movements

ERIC HOFFER

HARPER**PERENNIAL** MODERN**CLASSICS**

NEW YORK • LONDON • TORONTO • SYDNEY • NEW DELHI • AUCKLAND

To

MARGARET ANDERSON
without whose goading finger
which reached me aross a continent
this book
would not have been written

HARPER**PERENNIAL** ⬤ MODERN**CLASSICS**

This book was originally published by Harper & Row, Publishers, Inc., in 1951.

HarperCollins books may be purchased for educational, business, or sales promotional use. For information, please e-mail the Special Markets Department at SPsales@harpercollins.com.

First Perennial Library edition published 1966. Reset 1989.
First Perennial Modern Classics edition published 2002. Reissued 2010.

Library of Congress Cataloging-in-Publication Data

Hoffer, Eric.
   The true believer / Eric Hoffer—1st Perennial classics ed.
     p. cm.—(Perennial classics)
   Originally published: New York : Harper & Row, 1951.
   Includes bibliographical references.
   ISBN 978-0-06-050591-2
    1. Social groups. 2. Social psychology. 3. Fanaticism. 4. Social participation.
  I. Title. II. Perennial classic.

HM716 .H63 2002
303.48'4—dc21   2002072255

15 16 17   RRD   36 35 34 33 32

Man would fain be great and sees that he is little; would fain be happy and sees that he is miserable; would fain be perfect and sees that he is full of imperfections; would fain be the object of the love and esteem of men, and sees that his faults merit only their aversion and contempt. The embarrassment wherein he finds himself produces in him the most unjust and criminal passions imaginable, for he conceives a mortal hatred against that truth which blames him and convinces him of his faults.

—PASCAL, *Pensées*

And slime had they for mortar.

—GENESIS II

Contents

Preface   xi

PART 1. THE APPEAL OF MASS MOVEMENTS

I. The Desire for Change   3
II. The Desire for Substitutes   12
III. The Interchangeability of Mass Movements   16

PART 2. THE POTENTIAL CONVERTS

IV. The Role of the Undesirables in Human Affairs   24
V. The Poor   26
    The New Poor   26
    The Abjectly Poor   27
    The Free Poor   31
    The Creative Poor   34
    The Unified Poor   34
VI. Misfits   46
VII. The Inordinately Selfish   48

VIII. The Ambitious Facing Unlimited
Opportunities 49
IX. Minorities 50
X. The Bored 51
XI. The Sinners 53

PART 3. UNITED ACTION AND SELF-SACRIFICE

XII. Preface 58
XIII. Factors Promoting Self-sacrifice 62
Identification with a Collective
Whole 62
Make-believe 66
Deprecation of the Present 68
"Things Which Are Not" 76
Doctrine 79
Fanaticism 83
Mass Movements and Armies 88
XIV. Unifying Agents 91
Hatred 91
Imitation 101
Persuasion and Coercion 105
Leadership 111
Action 120
Suspicion 124
The Effects of Unification 126

PART 4. BEGINNING AND END

XV. Men of Words 130
XVI. The Fanatics 143
XVII. The Practical Men of Action 147
XVIII. Good and Bad Mass Movements 153
The Unattractiveness and Sterility
of the Active Phase 153

Some Factors Which Determine the
 Length of the Active Phase   157
Useful Mass Movements   162

Notes   169

Preface

This book deals with some peculiarities common to all mass movements, be they religious movements, social revolutions or nationalist movements. It does not maintain that all movements are identical, but that they share certain essential characteristics which give them a family likeness.

All mass movements generate in their adherents a readiness to die and a proclivity for united action; all of them, irrespective of the doctrine they preach and the program they project, breed fanaticism, enthusiasm, fervent hope, hatred and intolerance; all of them are capable of releasing a powerful flow of activity in certain departments of life; all of them demand blind faith and singlehearted allegiance.

All movements, however different in doctrine and aspiration, draw their early adherents from the same types of humanity; they all appeal to the same types of mind.

Though there are obvious differences between the fanatical Christian, the fanatical Mohammedan, the fanatical nationalist, the fanatical Communist and the fanatical Nazi, it is yet true that the fanaticism which animates them may be viewed and treated as one. The same is true of the force which drives them on to expansion and world dominion. There is a certain uniformity in all types of dedication, of faith, of pursuit of power, of unity and of self-sacrifice. There are vast differences in the contents of holy causes and doctrines, but a certain uniformity in the factors which make them effective. He who, like Pascal, finds precise reasons for the effectiveness of Christian doctrine has also found the reasons for the effectiveness of Communist, Nazi and nationalist doctrine. However different the holy causes people die for, they perhaps die basically for the same thing.

This book concerns itself chiefly with the active, revivalist phase of mass movements. This phase is dominated by the true believer—the man of fanatical faith who is ready to sacrifice his life for a holy cause—and an attempt is made to trace his genesis and outline his nature. As an aid in this effort, use is made of a working hypothesis. Starting out from the fact that the frustrated[1] predominate among the early adherents of all mass movements and that they usually join of their own accord, it is assumed: 1) that frustration of itself, without any proselytizing prompting from the outside, can generate most of the peculiar characteristics of the true believer; 2) that an effective technique of conversion consists basically in the inculcation and fixation of proclivities and responses indigenous to the frustrated mind.

To test the validity of these assumptions, it was necessary to inquire into the ills that afflict the frustrated, how they react against them, the degree to which these reactions correspond to the responses of the true believer, and, finally, the manner in which these reactions can facilitate the rise and spread of a mass movement. It was also necessary to examine the practices of contemporary movements, where successful techniques of conversion had been perfected and applied, in order to discover whether they corroborate the view that a proselytizing mass movement deliberately fosters in its adherents a frustrated state of mind, and that it automatically advances its interest when it seconds the propensities of the frustrated.

It is necessary for most of us these days to have some insight into the motives and responses of the true believer. For though ours is a godless age, it is the very opposite of irreligious. The true believer is everywhere on the march, and both by converting and antagonizing he is shaping the world in his own image. And whether we are to line up with him or against him, it is well that we should know all we can concerning his nature and potentialities.

It is perhaps not superfluous to add a word of caution. When we speak of the family likeness of mass movements, we use the word "family" in a taxonomical sense. The tomato and the nightshade are of the same family, the Solanaceae. Though the one is nutritious and the other poisonous, they have many morphological, anatomical and physiological traits in common so that even the non-botanist senses a family likeness. The assumption that mass movements have many traits in common does not imply that all movements are equally beneficent or poisonous. The book passes no judgments, and expresses no preferences. It merely tries to explain; and the explanations—all of them theories—are in the nature of suggestions and arguments even when they are stated in what seems a categorical tone. I can do no better than quote Montaigne: "All I say is by way of discourse, and nothing by way of advice. I should not speak so boldly if it were my due to be believed."

PART 1

The Appeal of Mass Movements

I

The Desire for Change

1

It is a truism that many who join a rising revolutionary movement are attracted by the prospect of sudden and spectacular change in their conditions of life. A revolutionary movement is a conspicuous instrument of change.

Not so obvious is the fact that religious and nationalist movements too can be vehicles of change. Some kind of widespread enthusiasm or excitement is apparently needed for the realization of vast and rapid change, and it does not seem to matter whether the exhilaration is derived from an expectation of untold riches or is generated by an active mass movement. In this country the spectacular changes since the Civil War were enacted in an atmosphere charged with the enthusiasm born of fabulous opportunities for self-advancement. Where self-advancement cannot, or is not allowed to, serve as a driving force, other sources of enthusiasm have to be found if momentous changes, such as the awakening and renovation of a stagnant society or radical reforms in the character and pattern of life of a community, are to be realized and perpetuated. Religious, revolutionary and nationalist movements are such generating plants of general enthusiasm.

In the past, religious movements were the conspicuous vehicles of change. The conservatism of a religion—its orthodoxy—is the inert coagulum of a once highly reactive sap. A rising religious movement is all change and experiment—open to new views and techniques from all quarters. Islam when it emerged was an organizing and modernizing medium. Christianity was a civilizing and modernizing influence among the savage tribes of Europe. The Crusades and the Reformation both were crucial factors in shaking the Western world from the stagnation of the Middle Ages.

In modern times, the mass movements involved in the realization of vast and rapid change are revolutionary and nationalist—singly or in combination. Peter the Great was probably the equal, in dedication, power and ruthlessness, of many of the most successful revolutionary or nationalist leaders. Yet he failed in his chief purpose, which was to turn Russia into a Western nation. And the reason he failed was that he did not infuse the Russian masses with some soul-stirring enthusiasm. He either did not think it necessary or did not know how to make of his purpose a holy cause. It is not strange that the Bolshevik revolutionaries who wiped out the last of the Czars and Romanovs should have a sense of kinship with Peter—a Czar and a Romanov. For his purpose is now theirs, and they hope to succeed where he failed. The Bolshevik revolution may figure in history as much an attempt to modernize a sixth of the world's surface as an attempt to build a Communist economy.

The fact that both the French and the Russian revolutions turned into nationalist movements seems to indicate that in modern times nationalism is the most copious and durable source of mass enthusiasm, and that nationalist fervor must be tapped if the drastic changes projected and initiated by revolutionary enthusiasm are to be consummated. One wonders whether the difficulties encountered by the present Labor government in Britain are not partly due to the fact that the attempt to change the economy of the country and the way of life of 49,000,000 people has been initiated in an atmosphere singularly free from fervor, exaltation and wild hope. The revulsion from the ugly patterns developed by most contemporary mass movements has kept the civilized and decent leaders of the Labor party shy of revolutionary enthusiasm. The possibility still remains that events might force them to make use of some mild form of chauvinism so that in Britain too "the socialization of the nation [might have] as its natural corollary the nationalization of socialism."[1]

The phenomenal modernization of Japan would probably not have been possible without the revivalist spirit of Japanese nationalism. It is perhaps also true that the rapid modernization of some European countries (Germany in particular) was facilitated to some extent by the upsurge and thorough diffusion of nationalist fervor. Judged by present indications, the renascence of Asia will be brought about through the instrumentality of nationalist movements rather than by other mediums. It was the rise of a genuine nationalist movement which enabled Kemal Atatürk to modernize Turkey almost overnight. In Egypt, untouched by a mass movement, modernization is slow and faltering, though its rulers, from the day of Mehmed Ali, have welcomed Western ideas, and its contacts with the West have been many and intimate. Zionism is an instrument for the renovation of a backward country and the transformation of shopkeepers and brain workers into farmers, laborers and soldiers. Had Chiang Kai-shek known how to set in motion a genuine mass movement, or at least sustain the nationalist enthusiasm kindled by the Japanese invasion, he might have been acting now as the renovator of China. Since he did not know how, he was easily shoved aside by the masters of the art of "religiofi-cation"—the art of turning practical purposes into holy causes. It is not difficult to see why America and Britain (or any Western democracy) could not play a direct and leading role in rousing the Asiatic countries from their backwardness and stagnation: the democracies are nei-ther inclined nor perhaps able to kindle a revivalist spirit in Asia's millions. The contribution of the Western democ-racies to the awakening of the East has been indirect and certainly unintended. They have kindled an enthusiasm of resentment against the West; and it is this anti-Western fervor which is at present rousing the Orient from its stag-nation of centuries.[2]

Though the desire for change is not infrequently a super-ficial motive, it is yet worth finding out whether a probing of this desire might not shed some light on the inner work-ing of mass movements. We shall inquire therefore into the nature of the desire for change.

2

There is in us a tendency to locate the shaping forces of our existence outside ourselves. Success and failure are unavoidably related in our minds with the state of things around us. Hence it is that people with a sense of fulfill-ment think it a good world and would like to conserve it as it is, while the frustrated favor radical change. The tendency to look for all causes outside ourselves persists even when it is clear that our state of being is the product of personal qualities such as ability, character, appear-ance, health and so on. "If anything ail a man," says Tho-reau, "so that he does not perform his functions, if he have a pain in his bowels even . . . he forthwith sets about reforming—the world."[3]

It is understandable that those who fail should incline

to blame the world for their failure. The remarkable thing is that the successful, too, however much they pride themselves on their foresight, fortitude, thrift and other "sterling qualities," are at bottom convinced that their success is the result of a fortuitous combination of circumstances. The self-confidence of even the consistently successful is never absolute. They are never sure that they know all the ingredients which go into the making of their success. The outside world seems to them a precariously balanced mechanism, and so long as it ticks in their favor they are afraid to tinker with it. Thus the resistance to change and the ardent desire for it spring from the same conviction, and the one can be as vehement as the other.

3

Discontent by itself does not invariably create a desire for change. Other factors have to be present before discontent turns into disaffection. One of these is a sense of power.

Those who are awed by their surroundings do not think of change, no matter how miserable their condition. When our mode of life is so precarious as to make it patent that we cannot control the circumstances of our existence, we tend to stick to the proven and the familiar. We counteract a deep feeling of insecurity by making of our existence a fixed routine. We hereby acquire the illusion that we have tamed the unpredictable. Fisherfolk, nomads and farmers who have to contend with the willful elements, the creative worker who depends on inspiration, the savage awed by his surroundings—they all fear change. They face the world as they would an all-powerful jury. The abjectly poor, too, stand in awe of the world around them and are not hospitable to change. It is a dangerous life we live when hunger and cold are at our heels. There is thus a conservatism of the destitute as profound as the conservatism of the privileged, and the former is as much a factor in the perpetuation of a social order as the latter.

The men who rush into undertakings of vast change usually feel they are in possession of some irresistible power. The generation that made the French Revolution had an extravagant conception of the omnipotence of man's reason and the boundless range of his intelligence. Never, says de Tocqueville, had humanity been prouder of itself nor had it ever so much faith in its own omnipotence. And joined with this exaggerated self-confidence was a universal thirst for change which came unbidden to every mind.[4] Lenin and the Bolsheviks who plunged recklessly into the chaos of the creation of a new world had blind faith in the omnipotence of Marxist doctrine. The Nazis had nothing as potent as that doctrine, but they had faith in an infallible leader and also faith in a new technique. For it is doubtful whether National Socialism would have made such rapid progress if it had not been for the electrifying conviction that the new techniques of blitzkrieg and propaganda made Germany irresistible.

Even the sober desire for progress is sustained by faith—faith in the intrinsic goodness of human nature and in the omnipotence of science. It is a defiant and blasphemous faith, not unlike that held by the men who set out to build "a city and a tower, whose top may reach unto heaven" and who believed that "nothing will be restrained from them, which they have imagined to do."[5]

4

Offhand one would expect that the mere possession of power would automatically result in a cocky attitude toward the world and a receptivity to change. But it is not always so. The powerful can be as timid as the weak.

What seems to count more than possession of instruments of power is faith in the future. Where power is not joined with faith in the future, it is used mainly to ward off the new and preserve the status quo. On the other hand, extravagant hope, even when not backed by actual power, is likely to generate a most reckless daring. For the hopeful can draw strength from the most ridiculous sources of power—a slogan, a word, a button. No faith is potent unless it is also faith in the future; unless it has a millennial component. So, too, an effective doctrine: as well as being a source of power, it must also claim to be a key to the book of the future.[6]

Those who would transform a nation or the world cannot do so by breeding and captaining discontent or by demonstrating the reasonableness and desirability of the intended changes or by coercing people into a new way of life. They must know how to kindle and fan an extravagant hope. It matters not whether it be hope of a heavenly kingdom, of heaven on earth, of plunder and untold riches, of fabulous achievement or world dominion. If the Communists win Europe and a large part of the world, it will not be because they know how to stir up discontent or how to infect people with hatred, but because they know how to preach hope.

5

Thus the differences between the conservative and the radical seem to spring mainly from their attitude toward the future. Fear of the future causes us to lean against and cling to the present, while faith in the future renders us receptive to change. Both the rich and the poor, the strong and the weak, they who have achieved much or little can be afraid of the future. When the present seems so perfect that the most we can expect is its even continuation in the future, change can only mean deterioration. Hence men of outstanding achievement and those who live full, happy lives usually set their faces against drastic innovation. The conservatism of invalids and people past middle age stems, too, from fear of the future. They are on the lookout for signs of decay, and feel that any change is more likely to be for the worse than for the better. The abjectly poor also are without faith in the future. The future seems to them a booby trap buried on the road ahead. One must step gingerly. To change things is to ask for trouble.

As for the hopeful: it does not seem to make any difference who it is that is seized with a wild hope—whether it be an enthusiastic intellectual, a land-hungry farmer, a get-rich-quick speculator, a sober merchant or industrialist, a plain workingman or a noble lord—they all proceed recklessly with the present, wreck it if necessary, and create a new world. There can thus be revolutions by the privileged as well as by the underprivileged. The movement of enclosure in sixteenth and seventeenth century England was a revolution by the rich. The woolen industry rose to high prosperity, and grazing became more profitable than cropping. The landowners drove off their tenants, enclosed the commons and wrought profound changes in the social and economic texture of the country. "The lords and nobles were upsetting the social order, breaking down ancient law and custom, sometimes by means of violence, often by pressure and intimidation."[7] Another English revolution by the rich occurred at the end of the eighteenth and the beginning of the nineteenth century. It was the Industrial Revolution. The breathtaking potentialities of mechanization set the minds of manufacturers and merchants on fire. They began a revolution "as extreme and radical as ever inflamed the minds of sectarians,"[8] and in a relatively short time these respectable,

Godfearing citizens changed the face of England beyond recognition.

When hopes and dreams are loose in the streets, it is well for the timid to lock doors, shutter windows and lie low until the wrath has passed. For there is often a monstrous incongruity between the hopes, however noble and tender, and the action which follows them. It is as if ivied maidens and garlanded youths were to herald the four horsemen of the apocalypse.

6

For men to plunge headlong into an undertaking of vast change, they must be intensely discontented yet not destitute, and they must have the feeling that by the possession of some potent doctrine, infallible leader or some new technique they have access to a source of irresistible power. They must also have an extravagant conception of the prospects and potentialities of the future. Finally, they must be wholly ignorant of the difficulties involved in their vast undertaking. Experience is a handicap. The men who started the French Revolution were wholly without political experience. The same is true of the Bolsheviks, Nazis and the revolutionaries in Asia. The experienced man of affairs is a latecomer. He enters the movement when it is already a going concern. It is perhaps the Englishman's political experience that keeps him shy of mass movements.

II

The Desire for Substitutes

7

There is a fundamental difference between the appeal of a mass movement and the appeal of a practical organization. The practical organization offers opportunities for self-advancement, and its appeal is mainly to self-interest. On the other hand, a mass movement, particularly in its active, revivalist phase, appeals not to those intent on bolstering and advancing a cherished self, but to those who crave to be rid of an unwanted self. A mass movement attracts and holds a following not because it can satisfy the desire for self-advancement, but because it can satisfy the passion for self-renunciation.

People who see their lives as irremediably spoiled cannot find a worth-while purpose in self-advancement. The prospect of an individual career cannot stir them to a mighty effort, nor can it evoke in them faith and a single-minded dedication. They look on self-interest as on something tainted and evil; something unclean and unlucky. Anything undertaken under the auspices of the self seems to them foredoomed. Nothing that has its roots and reasons in the self can be good and noble. Their innermost craving is for a new life—a rebirth—or, failing this, a chance to acquire new elements of pride, confidence, hope, a sense of purpose and worth by an identification with a holy cause. An active mass movement offers them opportunities for both. If they join the movement as full converts they are reborn to a new life in its close-knit collective body, or if attracted as sympathizers they find elements of pride, confidence and purpose by identifying themselves with the efforts, achievements and prospects of the movement.

To the frustrated a mass movement offers substitutes either for the whole self or for the elements which make life bearable and which they cannot evoke out of their individual resources.

It is true that among the early adherents of a mass movement there are also adventurers who join in the hope that the movement will give a spin to their wheel of fortune and whirl them to fame and power. On the other hand, a degree of selfless dedication is sometimes displayed by those who join corporations, orthodox political parties and other practical organizations. Still, the fact remains that a practical concern cannot endure unless it can appeal to and satisfy self-interest, while the vigor and growth of a rising mass movement depend on its capacity to evoke and satisfy the passion for self-renunciation. When a mass movement begins to attract people who are interested in their individual careers, it is a sign that it has passed its vigorous stage; that it is no longer engaged in molding a new world but in possessing and preserving the present. It ceases then to be a movement and becomes an enterprise. According to Hitler, the more "posts and offices a movement has to hand out, the more inferior stuff it will attract, and in the end these political hangers-on overwhelm a successful party in such number that the honest fighter of former days no longer recognizes the old movement. . . . When this happens, the 'mission' of such a movement is done for."[1]

The nature of the complete substitute offered by conversion is discussed in the chapters on self-sacrifice and united action in Part 3. Here we shall deal with the partial substitutes.

8

Faith in a holy cause is to a considerable extent a substitute for the lost faith in ourselves.

9

The less justified a man is in claiming excellence for his own self, the more ready is he to claim all excellence for his nation, his religion, his race or his holy cause.

10

A man is likely to mind his own business when it is worth minding. When it is not, he takes his mind off his own meaningless affairs by minding other people's business.

This minding of other people's business expresses itself in gossip, snooping and meddling, and also in feverish interest in communal, national and racial affairs. In running away from ourselves we either fall on our neighbor's shoulder or fly at his throat.

11

The burning conviction that we have a holy duty toward others is often a way of attaching our drowning selves to a passing raft. What looks like giving a hand is often a holding on for dear life. Take away our holy duties and you leave our lives puny and meaningless. There is no doubt that in exchanging a self-centered for a selfless life we gain enormously in self-esteem. The vanity of the selfless, even those who practice utmost humility, is boundless.

12

One of the most potent attractions of a mass movement is its offering of a substitute for individual hope. This attraction is particularly effective in a society imbued with the idea of progress. For in the conception of progress, "tomorrow" looms large, and the frustration resulting from having nothing to look forward to is the more poignant. Hermann Rauschning says of pre-Hitlerian Germany that "The feeling of having come to the end of all things was one of the worst troubles we endured after that lost war."[2] In a modern society people can live without hope only when kept dazed and out of breath by incessant hustling. The despair brought by unemployment comes not only from the threat of destitution, but from the sudden view of a vast nothingness ahead. The unemployed are more likely to follow the peddlers of hope than the handers-out of relief.

Mass movements are usually accused of doping their followers with hope of the future while cheating them of the enjoyment of the present. Yet to the frustrated the present is irremediably spoiled. Comforts and pleasures cannot make it whole. No real content or comfort can ever arise in their minds but from hope.[3]

13

When our individual interests and prospects do not seem worth living for, we are in desperate need of something apart from us to live for. All forms of dedication, devotion, loyalty and self-surrender are in essence a desperate clinging to something which might give worth and meaning to our futile, spoiled lives. Hence the embracing of a substitute will necessarily be passionate and extreme. We can have qualified confidence in ourselves, but the faith we have in our nation, religion, race or holy cause has to be extravagant and uncompromising. A substitute embraced in moderation cannot supplant and efface the self we want to forget. We cannot be sure that we have something worth living for unless we are ready to die for it. This readiness to die is evidence to ourselves and others that what we had to take as a substitute for an irrevocably missed or spoiled first choice is indeed the best there ever was.

III

The Interchangeability of Mass Movements

14

When people are ripe for a mass movement, they are usually ripe for any effective movement, and not solely for one with a particular doctrine or program. In pre-Hitlerian Germany it was often a toss up whether a restless youth would join the Communists or the Nazis. In the overcrowded pale of Czarist Russia the simmering Jewish population was ripe both for revolution and Zionism. In the same family, one member would join the revolutionaries and the other the Zionists. Dr. Chaim Weizmann quotes a saying of his mother in those days: "Whatever happens, I shall be well off. If Shemuel [the revolutionary son] is right, we shall all be happy in Russia; and if Chaim [the Zionist] is right, then I shall go to live in Palestine."[1]

This receptivity to all movements does not always cease even after the potential true believer has become the ardent convert of a specific movement. Where mass movements are in violent competition with each other, there are not infrequent instances of converts—even the most zealous—shifting their allegiance from one to the other. A Saul turning into Paul is neither a rarity nor a miracle. In our day, each proselytizing mass movement seems to regard the zealous adherents of its antagonist as its own potential converts. Hitler looked on the German Communists as potential National Socialists: "The *petit bourgeois* Social-Democrat and the trade-union boss will never make a National Socialist, but the Communist always will."[2] Captain Röhm boasted that he could turn the reddest Communist into a glowing nationalist in four weeks.[3] On the other hand, Karl Radek looked on the Nazi Brown Shirts (S.A.) as a reserve for future Communist recruits.[4]

Since all mass movements draw their adherents from the same types of humanity and appeal to the same types of mind, it follows: (a) all mass movements are competitive, and the gain of one in adherents is the loss of all the others; (b) all mass movements are interchangeable. One mass movement readily transforms itself into another. A religious movement may develop into a social revolution or a nationalist movement; a social revolution, into militant nationalism or a religious movement; a nationalist movement into a social revolution or a religious movement.

15

It is rare for a mass movement to be wholly of one character. Usually it displays some facets of other types of movement, and sometimes it is two or three movements in one. The exodus of the Hebrews from Egypt was a slave revolt, a religious movement and a nationalist movement. The militant nationalism of the Japanese is essentially religious. The French Revolution was a new religion. It had "its dogma, the sacred principles of the Revolution—*Liberté at sainte égalité*. It had its form of worship, an adaptation of Catholic ceremonial, which was elaborated in connection with civic *fêtes*. It had its saints, the heroes and martyrs of liberty."[5] At the same time, the French Revolution was also a nationalist movement. The legislative assembly decreed in 1792 that altars should be raised everywhere bearing the inscription: "the citizen is born, lives and dies for *la Patrie.*"[6]

The religious movements of the Reformation had a revolutionary aspect which expressed itself in peasant uprisings, and were also nationalist movements. Said Luther: "In the eyes of the Italians we Germans are merely low Teutonic swine. They exploit us like charlatans and suck the country to the marrow. Wake up Germany!"[7]

The religious character of the Bolshevik and Nazi revolutions is generally recognized. The hammer and sickle and the swastika are in a class with the cross. The ceremonial of their parades is as the ceremonial of a religious procession. They have articles of faith, saints, martyrs and holy sepulchers. The Bolshevik and Nazi revolutions are also full-blown nationalist movements. The Nazi revolution had been so from the beginning, while the nationalism of the Bolsheviks was a late development.

Zionism is a nationalist movement and a social revolution. To the orthodox Jew it is also a religious movement. Irish nationalism has a deep religious tinge. The present mass movements in Asia are both nationalist and revolutionary.

16

The problem of stopping a mass movement is often a matter of substituting one movement for another. A social revolution can be stopped by promoting a religious or nationalist movement. Thus in countries where Catholicism has recaptured its mass movement spirit, it counteracts the spread of communism. In Japan it was nationalism that canalized all movements of social protest. In our South, the movement of racial solidarity acts as a preventive of social upheaval. A similar situation may be observed among the French in Canada and the Boers in South Africa.

This method of stopping one movement by substituting another for it is not always without danger, and it does not usually come cheap. It is well for those who hug the present and want to preserve it as it is not to play with mass movements. For it always fares ill with the present when a genuine mass movement is on the march. In pre-war Italy and Germany practical businessmen acted in an entirely "logical" manner when they encouraged a Fascist and a Nazi movement in order to stop communism. But in doing so, these practical and logical people promoted their own liquidation.

There are other safer substitutes for a mass movement. In general, any arrangement which either discourages atomistic individualism or facilitates self-forgetting or offers chances for action and new beginnings tends to counteract the rise and spread of mass movements. These subjects are dealt with in later chapters. Here we shall touch upon one curious substitute for mass movements, namely migration.

17

Emigration offers some of the things the frustrated hope to find when they join a mass movement, namely, change and a chance for a new beginning. The same types who swell the ranks of a rising mass movement are also likely to avail themselves of a chance to emigrate. Thus migration can serve as a substitute for a mass movement. It is plausible, for instance, that had the United States and the British Empire welcomed mass migration from Europe after the First World War, there might have been neither a Fascist nor a Nazi revolution. In this country, free and easy migration over a vast continent contributed to our social stability.

However, because of the quality of their human material, mass migrations are fertile ground for the rise of genuine mass movements. It is sometimes difficult to tell where a mass migration ends and a mass movement begins—and which came first. The migration of the Hebrews from Egypt developed into a religious and nationalist movement. The migrations of the barbarians in the declining days of the Roman Empire were more than mere shifts of population. The indications are that the barbarians were relatively few in number, but, once they invaded a country, they were joined by the oppressed and dissatisfied in all walks of life: "it was a social revolution started and masked by a superficial foreign conquest."[8]

Every mass movement is in a sense a migration—a movement toward a promised land; and, when feasible and expedient, an actual migration takes place. This happened in the case of the Puritans, Anabaptists, Mormons,

Dukhobors and Zionists. Migration, in the mass, strengthens the spirit and unity of a movement; and whether in the form of foreign conquest, crusade, pilgrimage or settlement of new land it is practiced by most active mass movements.

PART 2

The Potential Converts

IV

The Role of the Undesirables
in Human Affairs

18

There is a tendency to judge a race, a nation or any distinct group by its least worthy members. Though manifestly unfair, this tendency has some justification. For the character and destiny of a group are often determined by its inferior elements.

The inert mass of a nation, for instance, is in its middle section. The decent, average people who do the nation's work in cities and on the land are worked upon and shaped by minorities at both ends—the best and the worst.[1]

The superior individual, whether in politics, literature, science, commerce or industry, plays a large role in shaping a nation, but so do individuals at the other extreme—the failures, misfits, outcasts, criminals, and all those who have lost their footing, or never had one, in the ranks of respectable humanity. The game of history is usually played by the best and the worst over the heads of the majority in the middle.

The reason that the inferior elements of a nation can exert a marked influence on its course is that they are wholly without reverence toward the present. They see their lives and the present as spoiled beyond remedy and they are ready to waste and wreck both: hence their recklessness and their will to chaos and anarchy. They also crave to dissolve their spoiled, meaningless selves in some soul-stirring spectacular communal undertaking—hence their proclivity for united action. Thus they are among the early recruits of revolutions, mass migrations and of religious, racial and chauvinist movements, and they imprint their mark upon these upheavals and movements which shape a nation's character and history.

The discarded and rejected are often the raw material of a nation's future. The stone the builders reject becomes the cornerstone of a new world. A nation without dregs and malcontents is orderly, decent, peaceful and pleasant, but perhaps without the seed of things to come. It was not the irony of history that the undesired in the countries of Europe should have crossed an ocean to build a new world on this continent. Only they could do it.

19

Though the disaffected are found in all walks of life, they are most frequent in the following categories: (a) the poor, (b) misfits, (c) outcasts, (d) minorities, (e) adolescent youth, (f) the ambitious (whether facing insurmountable obstacles or unlimited opportunities), (g) those in the grip of some vice or obsession, (h) the impotent (in body or mind), (i) the inordinately selfish, (j) the bored, (k) the sinners.

Sections 20–42 deal with some of these types.

V

The Poor

THE NEW POOR

20

Not all who are poor are frustrated. Some of the poor stagnating in the slums of the cities are smug in their decay. They shudder at the thought of life outside their familiar cesspool. Even the respectable poor, when their poverty is of long standing, remain inert. They are awed by the immutability of the order of things. It takes a cataclysm—an invasion, a plague or some other communal disaster—to open their eyes to the transitoriness of the "eternal order."

It is usually those whose poverty is relatively recent, the "new poor," who throb with the ferment of frustration. The memory of better things is as fire in their veins. They are the disinherited and dispossessed who respond to every rising mass movement. It was the new poor in seventeenth century England who ensured the success of the Puritan Revolution. During the movement of enclosure (see Section 5) thousands of landlords drove off their tenants and turned their fields into pastures. "Strong and active peasants, enamored of the soil that nurtured them, were transformed into wageworkers or sturdy beggars; ... city streets were filled with paupers."[1] It was this mass of the dispossessed who furnished the recruits for Cromwell's new-model army.

In Germany and Italy the new poor coming from a ruined middle class formed the chief support of the Nazi and Fascist revolutions. The potential revolutionaries in present-day England are not the workers but the disinherited civil servants and businessmen. This class has a vivid memory of affluence and dominion and is not likely to reconcile itself to straitened conditions and political impotence.

There have been of late, both here and in other countries, enormous periodic increases of a new type of new poor, and their appearance undoubtedly has contributed to the rise and spread of contemporary mass movements. Until recently the new poor came mainly from the propertied classes, whether in cities or on the land, but lately, and perhaps for the first time in history, the plain workingman appears in this role.

So long as those who did the world's work lived on a level of bare subsistence, they were looked upon and felt themselves as the traditionally poor. They felt poor in good times and bad. Depressions, however severe, were not seen as aberrations and enormities. But with the wide diffusion of a high standard of living, depressions and the unemployment they bring assumed a new aspect. The present-day workingman in the Western world feels unemployment as a degradation. He sees himself disinherited and injured by an unjust order of things, and is willing to listen to those who call for a new deal.

THE ABJECTLY POOR

21

The poor on the borderline of starvation live purposeful lives. To be engaged in a desperate struggle for food and shelter is to be wholly free from a sense of futility. The goals are concrete and immediate. Every meal is a fulfillment; to go to sleep on a full stomach is a triumph; and every windfall a miracle. What need could they have for "an inspiring super-individual goal which would give meaning and dignity to their lives?" They are immune to the appeal of a mass movement. Angelica Balabanoff describes the effect of abject poverty on the revolutionary ardor of famous radicals who flocked to Moscow in the early days of the Bolshevik revolution. "Here I saw men and women who had lived all their lives for ideas, who had voluntarily renounced material advantages, liberty, happiness, and family affection for the realisation of their ideals—completely absorbed by the problem of hunger and cold."[2]

Where people toil from sunrise to sunset for a bare living, they nurse no grievances and dream no dreams. One of the reasons for the unrebelliousness of the masses in China is the inordinate effort required there to scrape together the means of the scantiest subsistence. The intensified struggle for existence "is a static rather than a dynamic influence."[3]

22

Misery does not automatically generate discontent, nor is the intensity of discontent directly proportionate to the degree of misery.

Discontent is likely to be highest when misery is bearable; when conditions have so improved that an ideal state seems almost within reach. A grievance is most poignant when almost redressed. De Tocqueville in his researches into the state of society in France before the revolution was struck by the discovery that "in no one of

the periods which have followed the Revolution of 1789
has the national prosperity of France augmented more
rapidly than it did in the twenty years preceding that
event."[4] He is forced to conclude that "the French found
their position the more intolerable the better it became."[5]
In both France and Russia the land-hungry peasants
owned almost exactly one-third of the agricultural land
at the outbreak of revolution, and most of that land was
acquired during the generation or two preceding the revolution.[6] It is not actual suffering but the taste of better
things which excites people to revolt. A popular
upheaval in Soviet Russia is hardly likely before the people get a real taste of the good life. The most dangerous
moment for the regime of the Politburo will be when a
considerable improvement in the economic conditions of
the Russian masses has been achieved and the iron totalitarian rule somewhat relaxed. It is of interest that the
assassination, in December 1934, of Stalin's close friend
Kirov happened not long after Stalin had announced the
successful end of the first Five-Year Plan and the beginning of a new prosperous, joyous era.

The intensity of discontent seems to be in inverse proportion to the distance from the object fervently desired.
This is true whether we move toward our goal or away
from it. It is true both of those who have just come
within sight of the promised land, and of the disinherited
who are still within sight of it; both of the about-to-be
rich, free, etcetera, and of the new poor and those recently enslaved.

23

Our frustration is greater when we have much and want
more than when we have nothing and want some. We are

less dissatisfied when we lack many things than when we seem to lack but one thing.

24

We dare more when striving for superfluities than for necessities. Often when we renounce superfluities we end up lacking in necessities.

25

There is a hope that acts as an explosive, and a hope that disciplines and infuses patience. The difference is between the immediate hope and the distant hope.

A rising mass movement preaches the immediate hope. It is intent on stirring its followers to action, and it is the around-the-corner brand of hope that prompts people to act. Rising Christianity preached the immediate end of the world and the kingdom of heaven around the corner; Mohammed dangled loot before the faithful; the Jacobins promised immediate liberty and equality; the early Bolsheviki promised bread and land; Hitler promised an immediate end to Versailles' bondage and work and action for all. Later, as the movement comes into possession of power, the emphasis is shifted to the distant hope—the dream and the vision. For an "arrived" mass movement is preoccupied with the preservation of the present, and it prizes obedience and patience above spontaneous action, and when we "hope for that we see not, then do we with patience wait for it."[7]

Every established mass movement has its distant hope, its brand of dope to dull the impatience of the masses and reconcile them with their lot in life. Stalinism is as much an opium of the people as are the established religions.[8]

THE FREE POOR

26

Slaves are poor; yet where slavery is widespread and long-established, there is little likelihood for the rise of a mass movement. The absolute equality among the slaves, and the intimate communal life in slave quarters, preclude individual frustration. In a society with an institution of slavery the troublemakers are the newly enslaved and the freed slaves. In the case of the latter it is the burden of freedom which is at the root of their discontent.

Freedom aggravates at least as much as it alleviates frustration. Freedom of choice places the whole blame of failure on the shoulders of the individual. And as freedom encourages a multiplicity of attempts, it unavoidably multiplies failure and frustration. Freedom alleviates frustration by making available the palliatives of action, movement, change and protest.

Unless a man has the talents to make something of himself, freedom is an irksome burden. Of what avail is freedom to choose if the self be ineffectual? We join a mass movement to escape individual responsibility, or, in the words of the ardent young Nazi, "to be free from freedom."[9] It was not sheer hypocrisy when the rank-and-file Nazis declared themselves not guilty of all the enormities they had committed. They considered themselves cheated and maligned when made to shoulder responsibility for obeying orders. Had they not joined the Nazi movement in order to be free from responsibility?

It would seem then that the most fertile ground for the propagation of a mass movement is a society with considerable freedom but lacking the palliatives of frustration. It was precisely because the peasants of eighteenth

century France, unlike the peasants of Germany and
Austria, were no longer serfs and already owned land
that they were receptive to the appeal of the French Revolution. Nor perhaps would there have been a Bolshevik
revolution if the Russian peasant had not been free for a
generation or more and had had a taste of the private
ownership of land.

27

Even the mass movements which rise in the name of freedom against an oppressive order do not realize individual
liberty once they start rolling. So long as a movement is
engaged in a desperate struggle with the prevailing order
or must defend itself against enemies within or without, its
chief preoccupation will be with unity and self-sacrifice,
which require the surrender of the individual's will, judgment and advantage. According to Robespierre, the revolutionary government was "the despotism of liberty
against tyranny."[10]

The important point is that in forgetting or postponing
individual liberty, the active mass movement does not
run counter to the inclinations of a zealous following.
Fanatics, says Renan, fear liberty more than they fear
persecution.[11] It is true that the adherents of a rising
movement have a strong sense of liberation even though
they live and breathe in an atmosphere of strict adherence to tenets and commands. This sense of liberation
comes from having escaped the burdens, fears and hope-
lessness of an untenable individual existence. It is this
escape which they feel as a deliverance and redemption.
The experience of vast change, too, conveys a sense of
freedom, even though the changes are executed in a
frame of strict discipline. It is only when the movement

has passed its active stage and solidified into a pattern of stable institutions that individual liberty has a chance to emerge. The shorter the active phase, the more will it seem that the movement itself, rather than its termination, made possible the emergence of individual freedom. This impression will be the more pronounced the more tyrannical the dispensation which the mass movement overthrew and supplanted.

28

Those who see their lives as spoiled and wasted crave equality and fraternity more than they do freedom. If they clamor for freedom, it is but freedom to establish equality and uniformity. The passion for equality is partly a passion for anonymity: to be one thread of the many which make up a tunic; one thread not distinguishable from the others.[12] No one can then point us out, measure us against others and expose our inferiority.

They who clamor loudest for freedom are often the ones least likely to be happy in a free society. The frustrated, oppressed by their shortcomings, blame their failure on existing restraints. Actually their innermost desire is for an end to the "free for all." They want to eliminate free competition and the ruthless testing to which the individual is continually subjected in a free society.

29

Where freedom is real, equality is the passion of the masses. Where equality is real, freedom is the passion of a small minority.

Equality without freedom creates a more stable social pattern than freedom without equality.

THE CREATIVE POOR

30

Poverty when coupled with creativeness is usually free of frustration. This is true of the poor artisan skilled in his trade and of the poor writer, artist and scientist in the full possession of creative powers. Nothing so bolsters our self-confidence and reconciles us with ourselves as the continuous ability to create; to see things grow and develop under our hand, day in, day out. The decline of handicrafts in modern times is perhaps one of the causes for the rise of frustration and the increased susceptibility of the individual to mass movements.

It is impressive to observe how with a fading of the individual's creative powers there appears a pronounced inclination toward joining a mass movement. Here the connection between the escape from an ineffectual self and a responsiveness to mass movements is very clear. The slipping author, artist, scientist—slipping because of a drying-up of the creative flow within—drifts sooner or later into the camps of ardent patriots, race mongers, uplift promoters and champions of holy causes. Perhaps the sexually impotent are subject to the same impulse. (The role of the noncreative in the Nazi movement is discussed in Section 111.)

THE UNIFIED POOR

31

The poor who are members of a compact group—a tribe, a closely knit family, a compact racial or religious group— are relatively free of frustration and hence almost immune to the appeal of a proselytizing mass movement. The less a person sees himself as an autonomous individual capable of shaping his own course and solely responsible for his station in life, the less likely is he to see his poverty as evidence of his own inferiority. A member of a compact group has a higher "revolting point" than an autonomous individual. It requires more misery and personal humiliation to goad him to revolt. The cause of revolution in a totalitarian society is usually a weakening of the totalitarian framework rather than resentment against oppression and distress.

The strong family ties of the Chinese probably kept them for ages relatively immune to the appeal of mass movements. "The European who 'dies for his country' has behaved in a manner that is unintelligible to a Chinaman [sic], because his family is not directly benefited—is, indeed, damaged by the loss of one of its members." On the other hand, he finds it understandable and honorable "when a Chinaman, in consideration of so much paid to his family, consents to be executed as a substitute for a condemned criminal."[13]

It is obvious that a proselytizing mass movement must break down all existing group ties if it is to win a considerable following. The ideal potential convert is the individual who stands alone, who has no collective body he can blend with and lose himself in and so mask the pettiness, meaninglessness and shabbiness of his individual existence. Where a mass movement finds the corporate pattern of family, tribe, country, etcetera, in a state of disruption and decay, it moves in and gathers the harvest. Where it finds the corporate pattern in good repair, it must attack and disrupt. On the other hand, when as in recent years in Russia we see the Bolshevik movement bolstering family solidarity and encouraging national, racial and religious cohesion, it is a sign that the movement has passed its dynamic phase, that it has already established its new pattern of life, and that its chief concern is to hold and preserve that which it has attained. In the rest of the world where communism is still a struggling movement, it does all it can to disrupt the family and discredit national, racial and religious ties.

32

The attitude of rising mass movements toward the family is of considerable interest. Almost all our contemporary movements showed in their early stages a hostile attitude toward the family, and did all they could to discredit and disrupt it. They did it by undermining the authority of the parents; by facilitating divorce; by taking over the responsibility for feeding, educating and entertaining the children; and by encouraging illegitimacy. Crowded housing, exile, concentration camps and terror also helped to weaken and break up the family. Still, not one of our contemporary movements was so outspoken in its antagonism toward the family as was early Christianity. Jesus minced no words: "For I am come to set a man at variance against his father, and the daughter against her mother, and the daughter in law against her mother in law. And a man's foes shall be they of his own household. He that loveth father or mother more than me is not worthy of me: and he that loveth son or daughter more than me, is not worthy of me."[14] When He was told that His mother and brothers were outside desiring to speak with Him He said: "Who is my mother? and who are my brethren? And he stretched forth his hand toward his disciples, and said, Behold my mother, and my brethren!"[15] When one of His disciples asked leave to go and bury his father, Jesus said to him: "Follow me; and let the dead bury their dead."[16] He seemed to sense the ugly family conflicts His movement was bound to provoke both by its proselytizing and by the fanatical hatred of its antagonists. "And the brother shall deliver up the brother to death, and the father the child: and the children shall rise up against their parents, and cause them to be put to death."[17] It is strange but true that he who preaches brotherly love also preaches against love of mother, father, brother, sister, wife and children. The Chinese sage Mo-Tzü who advocated brotherly love was rightly condemned by the Confucianists who cherished the family above all. They argued that the principle of universal love would dissolve the family and destroy society.[18] The proselytizer who comes and says "Follow me" is a family-wrecker, even though he is not conscious of any hostility toward the family and has not the least intention of weakening its solidarity. When St. Bernard preached, his influence was such that "mothers are said to have hid their sons from him, and wives their husbands, lest he should lure them away. He actually broke up so many homes that the abandoned wives formed a nunnery."[19]

As one would expect, a disruption of the family, whatever its causes, fosters automatically a collective spirit and creates a responsiveness to the appeal of mass movements.

The Japanese invasion undoubtedly weakened the compact family pattern of the Chinese and contributed to their recent increased responsiveness to both nationalism and communism. In the industrialized Western world the family is weakened and disrupted mainly by economic factors. Economic independence for women facilitates divorce. Economic independence for the young weakens parental authority and also hastens an early splitting up of the family group. The drawing power of large industrial centers on people living on farms and in small towns strains and breaks family ties. By weakening the family these factors contributed somewhat to the growth of the collective spirit in modern times.

Hitler's lunatic shifting of entire populations during the Second World War and his fantastic feats of extermination must have minced and scrambled millions of families in a large part of Europe. At the same time, the Anglo-American air raids, the expulsion of nine million Germans from the east and south of Europe and the delayed repatriation of German prisoners of war did to Germany what Hitler had done to Europe. It is difficult to see how, even under optimal economic and political conditions, a continent strewn with the odds and ends of families could settle into a normal conservative social pattern.

33

The discontent generated in backward countries by their contact with Western civilization is not primarily resentment against exploitation by domineering foreigners. It is rather the result of a crumbling or weakening of tribal solidarity and communal life.

The ideal of self-advancement which the civilizing West offers to backward populations brings with it the plague of individual frustration. All the advantages brought by the West are ineffectual substitutes for the sheltering and soothing anonymity of a communal existence. Even when the Westernized native attains personal success—becomes rich, or masters a respected profession—he is not happy. He feels naked and orphaned. The nationalist movements in the colonial countries are partly a striving after group existence and an escape from Western individualism.

The Western colonizing powers offer the native the gift of individual freedom and independence. They try to teach him self-reliance. What it all actually amounts to is individual isolation. It means the cutting off of an immature and poorly furnished individual from the corporate whole and releasing him, in the words of Khomiakov, "to the freedom of his own impotence."[20] The feverish desire to band together and coalesce into marching masses so manifest both in our homelands and in the countries we colonize is the expression of a desperate effort to escape this ineffectual, purposeless individual existence. It is very possible, therefore, that the present nationalist movements in Asia may lead—even without Russian influence—to a more or less collectivist rather than democratic form of society.

The policy of an exploiting colonial power should be to encourage communal cohesion among the natives. It should foster equality and a feeling of brotherhood among them. For by how much the ruled blend and lose themselves into a compact whole, by so much is softened the poignancy of their individual futility; and the process which transmutes misery into frustration and revolt is checked at the source. The device of "divide and rule" is ineffective when it aims at a weakening of all forms of cohesion among the ruled. The breaking up of a village community, a tribe or a nation into autonomous individuals does not eliminate or stifle the spirit of rebellion against the ruling power. An effective division is one that fosters a multiplicity of compact bodies—racial, religious or economic—vying with and suspicious of each other.

Even when a colonial power is wholly philanthropic and its sole aim is to bring prosperity and progress to a backward people, it must do all it can to preserve and reinforce the corporate pattern. It must not concentrate on the individual but inject the innovations and reforms into tribal or communal channels and let the tribe or the community progress as a whole. It is perhaps true that the successful modernization of a backward people can be brought about only within a strong framework of united action. The spectacular modernization of Japan was accomplished in an atmosphere charged with the fervor of united action and group consciousness.

Soviet Russia's advantage as a colonizing power—aside from her lack of racial bias—is that it comes with a ready-made and effective pattern of united action. It can disregard, and indeed deliberately sweep away, all existing group ties without the risk of breeding individual discontent and eventual revolt. For the sovietized native is not left struggling alone in a hostile world. He begins his new life as a member of a closely knit group more compact and communal than his former clan or tribe.

The device of encouraging communal cohesion as a preventive of colonial unrest can also be used to prevent labor unrest in the industrialized colonizing countries.

The employer whose only purpose is to keep his workers at their task and get all he can out of them is not likely to attain his goal by dividing them—playing off one worker against the other. It is rather in his interest that the workers should feel themselves part of a whole, and preferably a whole which comprises the employer, too. A vivid feeling of solidarity, whether racial, national or religious, is undoubtedly an effective means of preventing labor unrest. Even when the type of solidarity is such that it cannot comprise the employer, it nevertheless tends to promote labor contentment and efficiency. Experience shows that production is at its best when the workers feel and act as members of a team. Any policy that disturbs and tears apart the team is bound to cause severe trouble. "Incentive wage plans that offer bonuses to individual workers do more harm than good. . . . Group incentive plans in which the bonus is based on the work of the whole team, including the foreman . . . are much more likely to promote greater productivity and greater satisfaction on the part of the workers."[21]

34

A rising mass movement attracts and holds a following not by its doctrine and promises but by the refuge it offers from the anxieties, barrenness and meaninglessness of an individual existence. It cures the poignantly frustrated not by conferring on them an absolute truth or by remedying the difficulties and abuses which made their lives miserable, but by freeing them from their ineffectual selves—and it does this by enfolding and absorbing them into a closely knit and exultant corporate whole.

It is obvious, therefore, that, in order to succeed, a mass movement must develop at the earliest moment a compact corporate organization and a capacity to absorb and integrate all comers. It is futile to judge the viability of a new movement by the truth of its doctrine and the feasibility of its promises. What has to be judged is its corporate organization for quick and total absorption of the frustrated. Where new creeds vie with each other for the allegiance of the populace, the one which comes with the most perfected collective framework wins. Of all the cults and philosophies which competed in the Graeco-Roman world, Christianity alone developed from its inception a compact organization. "No one of its rivals possessed so powerful and coherent a structure as did the church. No other gave its adherents quite the same feeling of coming into a closely knit community."[22] The Bolshevik movement outdistanced all other Marxist movements in the race for power because of its tight collective organization. The National Socialist movement, too, won out over all the other folkish movements which pullulated in the 1920's, because of Hitler's early recognition that a rising mass movement can never go too far in advocating and promoting collective cohesion. He knew that the chief passion of the frustrated is "to belong," and that there cannot be too much cementing and binding to satisfy this passion.

35

The milieu most favorable for the rise and propagation of mass movements is one in which a once compact corporate structure is, for one reason or another, in a state of disintegration. The age in which Christianity rose and spread "was one when large numbers of men were uprooted. The compact city states had been partly merged into one vast empire . . . and the old social and political groupings had been weakened or dissolved."[23] Christianity made its greatest headway in the large cities where lived "thousands of deracinated individuals, some of them slaves, some freedmen, and some merchants, who had been separated by force or voluntarily from their hereditary milieu."[24] In the countryside where the communal pattern was least disturbed, the new religion found the ground less favorable. The villagers *(pagani)* and the heath-dwellers (heathen) clung longest to the ancient cults. A somewhat similar situation is to be observed in the rise of nationalist and socialist movements in the second half of the nineteenth century: "the extraordinary mobility and urbanization of population served to create during those decades an extraordinary number of . . . persons uprooted from ancestral soil and local allegiance. Experiencing grave economic insecurity and psychological maladjustment, these were very susceptible to demagogic propaganda, socialist or nationalist or both."[25]

The general rule seems to be that as one pattern of corporate cohesion weakens, conditions become ripe for the rise of a mass movement and the eventual establishment of a new and more vigorous form of compact unity. When a church which was all-embracing relaxes its hold, new religious movements are likely to crystallize. H. G. Wells remarks that at the time of the Reformation people "objected not to the church's power, but to its weaknesses. . . . Their movements against the church, within it and without, were movements not for release from a religious control, but for a fuller and more abundant religious control."[26] If the religious mood is undermined by enlightenment, the rising movements will be socialist, nationalist or racist. The French Revolution, which was also a nationalist movement, came as a reaction not against the vigorous tyranny of the Catholic Church and the ancient regime but against their weakness and ineffectuality. When people revolt in a totalitarian society, they rise not against the wickedness of the regime but its weakness.

Where the corporate pattern is strong, it is difficult for a mass movement to find a footing. The communal compactness of the Jews, both in Palestine and the Diaspora, was probably one of the reasons that Christianity made so little headway among them. The destruction of the temple caused, if anything, a tightening of the communal bonds. The synagogue and the congregation received now much of the devotion which formerly flowed toward the temple and Jerusalem. Later, when the Christian church had the power to segregate the Jews in ghettos, it gave their communal compactness an additional reinforcement, and thus, unintentionally, ensured the survival of Judaism intact through the ages. The coming of "enlightenment" undermined both orthodoxy and ghetto walls. Suddenly, and perhaps for the first time since the days of Job and Ecclesiastes, the Jew found himself an individual, terribly alone in a hostile world. There was no collective body he could blend with and lose himself in. The synagogue and the congregation had become shriveled lifeless things, while the traditions and prejudices of two thousand years prevented his complete integration with the Gentile corporate bodies. Thus the modern Jew became the most autonomous of individuals, and inevitably, too, the most frustrated. It is not surprising, therefore, that the mass movements of modern times often found in him a ready convert. The Jew also crowded the roads leading to palliatives of frustration, such as hustling and migration. He also threw himself into a passionate effort to prove his individual worth by material achievements and creative work. There was, it is true, one speck of corporateness he could create around himself by his own efforts, namely, the family— and he made the most of it. But in the case of the European Jew, Hitler chewed and scorched this only refuge in concentration camps and gas chambers. Thus now, more than ever before, the Jew, particularly in Europe, is the ideal potential convert. And it almost seems providential that Zionism should be on hand in the Jew's darkest hour to enfold him in its corporate embrace and cure him of his individual isolation. Israel is indeed a rare refuge: it is home and family, synagogue and congregation, nation and revolutionary party all in one.

The recent history of Germany also furnishes an interesting example of the relation between corporate compactness and a receptivity to the appeal of mass movements. There was no likelihood of a genuine revolutionary movement arising in Wilhelmian Germany. The Germans were satisfied with the centralized, authoritarian Kaiser regime, and even defeat in the First World War did not impair their love for it. The revolution of 1918 was an artificial thing with little popular backing. The years of the Weimar Constitution which followed were for most Germans a time of irritation and frustration. Used as they were to commands from above and respect for authority, they found the loose, irreverent democratic order all confusion and chaos. They were shocked to realize "that they had to participate in government, choose a party, and pass judgment upon political matters."[27] They longed for a new corporate whole, more monolithic, all-embracing and glorious to behold than even the Kaiser regime had been—and the Third Reich more than answered their prayer. Hitler's totalitarian regime, once established, was never in danger of mass revolt. So long as the ruling Nazi hierarchy was willing to shoulder all responsibilities and make all decisions, there was not the least chance for any popular antagonism to arise. A danger point could have been reached had Nazi discipline and its totalitarian control been relaxed. What de Tocqueville says of a tyrannical government is true of all totalitarian orders—their moment of greatest danger is when they begin to reform, that is to say, when they begin to show liberal tendencies.[28]

Another and final illustration of the thesis that effective collective bodies are immune to the appeal of mass movements but that a crumbling collective pattern is the most favorable milieu for their rise is found in the relation between the collective body we know as an army and mass movements. There is hardly an instance of an intact army giving rise to a religious, revolutionary or nationalist movement. On the other hand, a distintegrating army—whether by the orderly process of demobilization or by desertion due to demoralization—is fertile ground for a proselytizing movement. The man just out of the army is an ideal potential convert, and we find him among the early adherents of all contemporary mass movements. He feels alone and lost in the free-for-all of civilian life. The responsibilities and uncertainties of an autonomous existence weigh and prey upon him. He longs for certitude, camaraderie, freedom from individual responsibility, and a vision of something altogether different from the competitive free society around him—and he finds all this in the brotherhood and the revivalist atmosphere of a rising movement.[29]

VI

Misfits

36

The frustration of misfits can vary in intensity. There are first the temporary misfits: people who have not found their place in life but still hope to find it. Adolescent youth, unemployed college graduates, veterans, new immigrants and the like are of this category. They are restless, dissatisfied and haunted by the fear that their best years will be wasted before they reach their goal. They are receptive to the preaching of a proselytizing movement and yet do not always make staunch converts. For they are not irrevocably estranged from the self; they do not see it as irremediably spoiled. It is easy for them to conceive an autonomous existence that is purposeful and hopeful. The slightest evidence of progress and success reconciles them with the world and their selves.

The role of veterans in the rise of mass movements has been touched upon in Section 35. A prolonged war by national armies is likely to be followed by a period of social unrest for victors and vanquished alike. The reason is neither the unleashing of passions and the taste of violence during wartime nor the loss of faith in a social order that could not prevent so enormous and meaningless a waste of life and wealth. It is rather due to the prolonged break in the civilian routine of the millions enrolled in the national armies. The returning soldiers find it difficult to recapture the rhythm of their prewar lives. The readjustment to peace and home is slow and painful, and the country is flooded with temporary misfits.

Thus it seems that the passage from war to peace is more critical for an established order than the passage from peace to war.

37

The permanent misfits are those who because of a lack of talent or some irreparable defect in body or mind cannot do the one thing for which their whole being craves. No achievement, however spectacular, in other fields can give them a sense of fulfillment. Whatever they undertake becomes a passionate pursuit; but they never arrive, never pause. They demonstrate the fact that we can never have enough of that which we really do not want, and that we run fastest and farthest when we run from ourselves.

The permanent misfits can find salvation only in a complete separation from the self; and they usually find it by losing themselves in the compact collectivity of a mass movement. By renouncing individual will, judgment and ambition, and dedicating all their powers to the service of an eternal cause, they are at last lifted off the endless treadmill which can never lead them to fulfillment.

The most incurably frustrated—and, therefore, the most vehement—among the permanent misfits are those with an unfulfilled craving for creative work. Both those who try to write, paint, compose, etcetera, and fail decisively, and those who after tasting the elation of creativeness feel a drying up of the creative flow within and know that never again will they produce aught worth-while, are alike in the grip of a desperate passion. Neither fame nor power nor riches nor even monumental achievements in other fields can still their hunger. Even the wholehearted dedication to a holy cause does not always cure them. Their unappeased hunger persists, and they are likely to become the most violent extremists in the service of their holy cause.[1]

VII

The Inordinately Selfish

38

The inordinately selfish are particularly susceptible to frustration. The more selfish a person, the more poignant his disappointments. It is the inordinately selfish, therefore, who are likely to be the most persuasive champions of selflessness.

The fiercest fanatics are often selfish people who were forced, by innate shortcomings or external circumstances, to lose faith in their own selves. They separate the excellent instrument of their selfishness from their ineffectual selves and attach it to the service of some holy cause. And though it be a faith of love and humility they adopt, they can be neither loving nor humble.

VIII

The Ambitious Facing
Unlimited Opportunities

39

Unlimited opportunities can be as potent a cause of frustration as a paucity or lack of opportunities. When opportunities are apparently unlimited, there is an inevitable deprecation of the present. The attitude is: "All that I am doing or possibly can do is chicken feed compared with what is left undone." Such is the frustration which broods over gold camps and haunts taut minds in boom times. Hence the remarkable fact that, joined with the ruthless self-seeking which seems to be the mainspring of gold-hunters, land-grabbers and other get-rich-quick enthusiasts, there is an excessive readiness for self-sacrifice and united action. Patriotism, racial solidarity, and even the preaching of revolution find a more ready response among people who see limitless opportunities spread out before them than among those who move within the fixed limits of a familiar, orderly and predictable pattern of existence.

IX

Minorities

40

A minority is in a precarious position, however protected it be by law or force. The frustration engendered by the unavoidable sense of insecurity is less intense in a minority intent on preserving its identity than in one bent upon dissolving in and blending with the majority. A minority which preserves its identity is inevitably a compact whole which shelters the individual, gives him a sense of belonging and immunizes him against frustration. On the other hand, in a minority bent on assimilation, the individual stands alone, pitted against prejudice and discrimination. He is also burdened with the sense of guilt, however vague, of a renegade. The orthodox Jew is less frustrated than the emancipated Jew. The segregated Negro in the South is less frustrated than the nonsegregated Negro in the North.

Again, within a minority bent on assimilation, the least and most successful (economically and culturally) are likely to be more frustrated than those in between. The man who fails sees himself as an outsider; and, in the case of a member of a minority group who wants to blend with the majority, failure intensifies the feeling of not belonging. A similar feeling crops up at the other end of the economic or cultural scale. Those of a minority who attain fortune and fame often find it difficult to gain entrance into the exclusive circles of the majority. They are thus made conscious of their foreignness. Furthermore, having evidence of their individual superiority, they resent the admission of inferiority implied in the process of assimilation. Thus it is to be expected that the least and most successful of a minority bent on assimilation should be the most responsive to the appeal of a proselytizing mass movement. The least and most successful among the Italian Americans were the most ardent admirers of Mussolini's revolution; the least and most successful among the Irish Americans were the most responsive to De Valera's call; the least and most successful among the Jews are the most responsive to Zionism; the least and most successful among the Blacks are the most race conscious.

X

The Bored

41

There is perhaps no more reliable indicator of a society's ripeness for a mass movement than the prevalence of unrelieved boredom. In almost all the descriptions of the periods preceding the rise of mass movements there is reference to vast ennui; and in their earliest stages mass movements are more likely to find sympathizers and support among the bored than among the exploited and oppressed. To a deliberate fomenter of mass upheavals, the report that people are bored stiff should be at least as encouraging as that they are suffering from intolerable economic or political abuses.

When people are bored, it is primarily with their own selves that they are bored. The consciousness of a barren, meaningless existence is the main fountainhead of boredom. People who are not conscious of their individual separateness, as is the case with those who are members of a compact tribe, church, party, etcetera, are not accessible to boredom. The differentiated individual is free of boredom only when he is engaged either in creative work or some absorbing occupation or when he is wholly engrossed in the struggle for existence. Pleasure-chasing and dissipation are ineffective palliatives. Where people live autonomous lives and are not badly off, yet are without abilities or opportunities for creative work or useful action, there is no telling to what desperate and fantastic shifts they might resort in order to give meaning and purpose to their lives.

Boredom accounts for the almost invariable presence of spinsters and middle-aged women at the birth of mass movements. Even in the case of Islam and the Nazi movement, which frowned upon feminine activity outside the home, we find women of a certain type playing an important role in the early stage of their development.

Marriage has for women many equivalents of joining a mass movement. It offers them a new purpose in life, a new future and a new identity (a new name). The boredom of spinsters and of women who can no longer find joy and fulfillment in marriage stems from an awareness of a barren, spoiled life. By embracing a holy cause and dedicating their energies and substance to its advancement, they find a new life full of purpose and meaning. Hitler made full use of "the society ladies thirsting for adventure, sick of their empty lives, no longer getting a 'kick' out of love affairs."[1] He was financed by the wives of some of the great industrialists long before their husbands had heard of him.[2] Miriam Beard tells of a similar role played by bored wives of businessmen before the French Revolution: "they were devastated with boredom and given to fits of the vapors. Restlessly, they applauded innovators."[3]

XI

The Sinners

42

The sardonic remark that patriotism is the last refuge of scoundrels has also a less derogatory meaning. Fervent patriotism as well as religious and revolutionary enthusiasm often serves as a refuge from a guilty conscience. It is a strange thing that both the injurer and the injured, the sinner and he who is sinned against, should find in the mass movement an escape from a blemished life. Remorse and a sense of grievance seem to drive people in the same direction.

It sometimes seems that mass movements are custom-made to fit the needs of the criminal—not only for the catharsis of his soul but also for the exercise of his inclinations and talents. The technique of a proselytizing mass movement aims to evoke in the faithful the mood and frame of mind of a repentant criminal.[1] Self-surrender, which is, as will be shown in Part 3, the source of a mass movement's unity and vigor, is a sacrifice, an act of atonement, and clearly no atonement is called for unless there is a poignant sense of sin. Here, as elsewhere, the technique of a mass movement aims to infect people with a malady and then offer the movement as a cure. "What a task confronts the American clergy"—laments an American divine—"preaching the good news of a Savior to people who for the most part have no real sense of sin."[2] An effective mass movement cultivates the idea of sin. It depicts the autonomous self not only as barren and helpless but also as vile. To confess and repent is to slough off one's individual distinctness and separateness, and salvation is found by losing oneself in the holy oneness of the congregation.[3]

There is a tender spot for the criminal and an ardent wooing of him in all mass movements. St. Bernard, the moving spirit of the Second Crusade, thus appealed for recruits: "For what is it but an exquisite and priceless chance of salvation due to God alone, that the omnipotent should deign to summon to His service, as though they were innocent, murderers, ravishers, adulterers, perjurers, and those guilty of every crime?"[4] Revolutionary Russia too has a tender spot for the common criminal, though it is ruthless with the heretic—the ideological "deviationist." It is perhaps true that the criminal who embraces a holy cause is more ready to risk his life and go to extremes in its defense than people who are awed by the sanctity of life and property.

Crime is to some extent a substitute for a mass movement. Where public opinion and law enforcement are not too stringent, and poverty not absolute, the underground pressure of malcontents and misfits often leaks out in crime. It has been observed that in the exaltation of mass movements (whether patriotic, religious or revolutionary) common crime declines.

PART 3

United Action and Self-Sacrifice

XII

Preface

43

The vigor of a mass movement stems from the propensity of its followers for united action and self-sacrifice. When we ascribe the success of a movement to its faith, doctrine, propaganda, leadership, ruthlessness and so on, we are but referring to instruments of unification and to means used to inculcate a readiness for self-sacrifice. It is perhaps impossible to understand the nature of mass movements unless it is recognized that their chief preoccupation is to foster, perfect and perpetuate a facility for united action and self-sacrifice. To know the processes by which such a facility is engendered is to grasp the inner logic of most of the characteristic attitudes and practices of an active mass movement. With few exceptions,[1] any group or organization which tries, for one reason or another, to create and maintain compact unity and a constant readiness for self-sacrifice usually manifests the peculiarities—both noble and base—of a mass movement. On the other hand, a mass movement is bound to lose much which distinguishes it from other types of organization when it relaxes its collective compactness and begins to countenance self-interest as a legitimate motive of activity. In times of peace and prosperity, a democratic nation is an institutionalized association of more or less free individuals. On the other hand, in time of crisis, when the nation's existence is threatened, and it tries to reinforce its unity and generate in its people a readiness for self-sacrifice, it almost always assumes in some degree the character of a mass movement. The same is true of religious and revolutionary organizations: whether or not they develop into mass movements depends less on the doctrine they preach and the program they project than on the degree of their preoccupation with unity and the readiness for self-sacrifice.

The important point is that in the poignantly frustrated the propensities for united action and self-sacrifice arise spontaneously. It should be possible, therefore, to gain some clues concerning the nature of these propensities, and the technique to be employed for their deliberate inculcation, by tracing their spontaneous emergence in the frustrated mind. What ails the frustrated? It is the consciousness of an irremediably blemished self. Their chief desire is to escape that self—and it is this desire which manifests itself in a propensity for united action and self-sacrifice. The revulsion from an unwanted self, and the impulse to forget it, mask it, slough it off and lose it, produce both a readiness to sacrifice the self and a willingness to dissolve it by losing one's individual distinctness in a compact collective whole. Moreover, the estrangement from the self is usually accompanied by a train of diverse and seemingly unrelated attitudes and impulses which a closer probing reveals to be essential factors in the process of unification and of self-sacrifice. In other words, frustration not only gives rise to the desire for unity and the readiness for self-sacrifice but also creates a mechanism for their realization. Such diverse phenomena as a deprecation of the present, a facility for make-believe, a proneness to hate, a readiness to imitate, credulity, a readiness to attempt the impossible, and many others which crowd the minds of the intensely frustrated are, as we shall see, unifying agents and prompters of recklessness.

In Sections 44–103 an attempt will be made to show that when we set out to inculcate in people a facility for united action and self-sacrifice, we do all we can—whether we know it or not—to induce and encourage an estrangement from the self, and that we strive to evoke and cultivate in them many of the diverse attitudes and impulses which accompany the spontaneous estrangement from the self in the frustrated. In short, we shall try to show that the technique of an active mass movement consists basically in the inculcation and cultivation of proclivities and responses indigenous to the frustrated mind.

The reader is expected to quarrel with much that is said in this part of the book. He is likely to feel that much has been exaggerated and much ignored. But this is not an authoritative textbook. It is a book of thoughts, and it does not shy away from half-truths so long as they seem to hint at a new approach and help to formulate new questions. "To illustrate a principle," says Bagehot, "you must exaggerate much and you must omit much."

The capacities for united action and self-sacrifice seem almost always to go together. When we hear of a group that is particularly contemptuous of death, we are usually justified in concluding that the group is closely knit and thoroughly unified.[2] On the other hand, when we face a member of a compact group, we are likely to find him contemptuous of death. Both united action and self-sacrifice require self-diminution. In order to become part of a compact whole, the individual has to forego much. He has to give up privacy, individual judgment and often individual possessions. To school a person to united action is, therefore, to ready him for acts of self-denial. On the other hand, the man who practices self-abnegation sloughs off the hard shell which keeps him apart from others and is thus made assimilable. Every unifying agent is, therefore, a promoter of self-sacrifice and vice versa. Nevertheless, in the following sections, a division is made for the sake of convenience. But the dual function of each factor is always kept in mind.

It is well to outline here the plan followed in Sections 44–63, which deal with the subject of self-sacrifice.

The technique of fostering a readiness to fight and to die consists in separating the individual from his flesh-and-blood self—in not allowing him to be his real self. This can be achieved by the thorough assimilation of the individual into a compact collective body—Sections 44–46; by endowing him with an imaginary self (make-believe)—Section 47; by implanting in him a deprecating attitude toward the present and riveting his interest on things that are not yet—Sections 48–55; by interposing a fact-proof screen between him and reality (doctrine)—Sections 56–59; by preventing, through the injection of passions, the establishment of a stable equilibrium between the individual and his self (fanaticism)—Sections 60–63.

XIII

Factors Promoting Self-sacrifice

IDENTIFICATION WITH A
COLLECTIVE WHOLE

44

To ripen a person for self-sacrifice he must be stripped of his individual identity and distinctness. He must cease to be George, Hans, Ivan, or Tadao—a human atom with an existence bounded by birth and death. The most drastic way to achieve this end is by the complete assimilation of the individual into a collective body. The fully assimilated individual does not see himself and others as human beings. When asked who he is, his automatic response is that he is a German, a Russian, a Japanese, a Christian, a Moslem, a member of a certain tribe or family. He has no purpose, worth and destiny apart from his collective body; and as long as that body lives he cannot really die.

To a man utterly without a sense of belonging, mere life is all that matters. It is the only reality in an eternity of nothingness, and he clings to it with shameless despair. Dostoyevsky gave words to this state of mind in *Crime and Punishment* (Part II, Chapter 4). The student Raskolnikov wanders about the streets of St. Petersburg in a delirious state. He had several days ago murdered two old women with an ax. He feels cut off from mankind. As he passes through the red-light district near the Hay Market he muses: "if one had to live on some high rock on such a narrow ledge that he'd only room to stand, and the ocean, everlasting darkness, everlasting solitude, everlasting tempest around him, if he had to remain standing on a square yard of space all his life, a thousand years, eternity, it were better to live so than to die at once! Only to live, to live and live! Life whatever it may be!"

The effacement of individual separateness must be thorough. In every act, however trivial, the individual must by some ritual associate himself with the congregation, the tribe, the party, etcetera. His joys and sorrows, his pride and confidence must spring from the fortunes and capacities of the group rather than from his individual prospects and abilities. Above all, he must never feel alone. Though stranded on a desert island, he must still feel that he is under the eyes of the group. To be cast out from the group should be equivalent to being cut off from life.

This is undoubtedly a primitive state of being, and its most perfect examples are found among primitive tribes. Mass movements strive to approximate this primitive perfection, and we are not imagining things when the antiindividualist bias of contemporary mass movements strikes us as a throwback to the primitive.

45

The capacity to resist coercion stems partly from the individual's identification with a group. The people who stood up best in the Nazi concentration camps were those who felt themselves members of a compact party (the Communists), of a church (priests and ministers), or of a close-knit national group. The individualists, whatever their nationality, caved in. The Western European Jew proved to be the most defenseless. Spurned by the Gentiles (even those within the concentration camps), and without vital ties with a Jewish community, he faced his tormentors alone—forsaken by the whole of humanity. One realizes now that the ghetto of the Middle Ages was for the Jews more a fortress than a prison. Without the sense of utmost unity and distinctness which the ghetto imposed upon them, they could not have endured with unbroken spirit the violence and abuse of those dark centuries. When the Middle Ages returned for a brief decade in our day, they caught the Jew without his ancient defenses and crushed him.

The unavoidable conclusion seems to be that when the individual faces torture or annihilation, he cannot rely on the resources of his own individuality. His only source of strength is in not being himself but part of something mighty, glorious and indestructible. Faith here is primarily a process of identification; the process by which the individual ceases to be himself and becomes part of something eternal. Faith in humanity, in posterity, in the destiny of one's religion, nation, race, party or family—what is it but the visualization of that eternal something to which we attach the self that is about to be annihilated?

It is somewhat terrifying to realize that the totalitarian leaders of our day, in recognizing this source of desperate courage, made use of it not only to steel the spirit of their followers but also to break the spirit of their opponents. In his purges of the old Bolshevik leaders, Stalin succeeded in turning proud and brave men into cringing cowards by depriving them of any possibility of identification with the party they had served all their lives and with the Russian masses. These old Bolsheviks had long ago cut themselves off from humanity outside Russia. They had an unbounded contempt for the past and for history which could still be made by capitalistic humanity. They had renounced God. There was for them neither past nor future, neither memory nor glory outside the confines of holy

Russia and the Communist party—and both these were now wholly and irrevocably in Stalin's hands. They felt themselves, in the words of Bukharin, "isolated from everything that constitutes the essence of life." So they confessed. By humbling themselves before the congregation of the faithful they broke out of their isolation. They renewed their communion with the eternal whole by reviling the self, accusing it of monstrous and spectacular crimes and sloughing it off in public.

The same Russians who cringe and crawl before Stalin's secret police displayed unsurpassed courage when facing—singly or in a group—the invading Nazis. The reason for this contrasting behavior is not that Stalin's police are more ruthless than Hitler's armies, but that when facing Stalin's police the Russian feels a mere individual while, when facing the Germans, he saw himself a member of a mighty race, possessed of a glorious past and even more glorious future.

Similarly, in the case of the Jews, their behavior in Palestine could not have been predicted from their behavior in Europe. The British colonial officials in Palestine followed a policy sound in logic but lacking in insight. They reasoned that since Hitler had managed to exterminate six million Jews without meeting serious resistance, it should not be too difficult to handle the 600,000 Jews in Palestine. Yet they found that the Jews in Palestine, however recently arrived, were a formidable enemy: reckless, stubborn and resourceful. The Jew in Europe faced his enemies alone, an isolated individual, a speck of life floating in an eternity of nothingness. In Palestine he felt himself not a human atom, but a member of an eternal race, with an immemorable past behind it and a breathtaking future ahead.

46

The theoreticians in the Kremlin are probably aware that
in order to maintain the submissiveness of the Russian
masses there must not be the least chance of an identification with any collective body outside Russia. The purpose of the Iron Curtain is perhaps more to prevent the
Russian people from reaching out—even in thought—toward an outside world, than to prevent the infiltration of
spies and saboteurs. The curtain is both physical and psychological. The complete elimination of any chance of
emigration—even of Russian citizens married to foreigners—blurs the awareness of outside humanity in Russian
minds. One might as well dream and hope of escaping to
another planet. The psychological barrier is equally important: the Kremlin's brazen propaganda strives to im-
press upon the Russians that there is nothing worthy and
eternal, nothing deserving of admiration and reverence,
nothing worth identifying oneself with, outside the confines of holy Russia.

MAKE-BELIEVE

47

Dying and killing seem easy when they are part of a ritual,
ceremonial, dramatic performance or game. There is need
for some kind of make-believe in order to face death un-
flinchingly. To our real, naked selves there is not a thing on
earth or in heaven worth dying for. It is only when we see
ourselves as actors in a staged (and therefore unreal) performance that death loses its frightfulness and finality and
becomes an act of make-believe and a theatrical gesture. It
is one of the main tasks of a real leader to mask the grim

reality of dying and killing by evoking in his followers the illusion that they are participating in a grandiose spectacle, a solemn or light-hearted dramatic performance.

Hitler dressed eighty million Germans in costumes and made them perform in a grandiose, heroic and bloody opera. In Russia, where even the building of a latrine involves some self-sacrifice, life has been an uninterrupted soul-stirring drama going on for thirty years, and its end is not yet. The people of London acted heroically under a hail of bombs because Churchill cast them in the role of heroes. They played their heroic role before a vast audience—ancestors, contemporaries and posterity—and on a stage lighted by a burning world city and to the music of barking guns and screaming bombs. It is doubtful whether in our contemporary world, with its widespread individual differentiation, any measure of general self-sacrifice can be realized without theatrical hocus-pocus and fireworks. It is difficult to see, therefore, how the present Labor government in England can realize its program of socialization, which demands some measure of self-sacrifice from every Briton, in the colorless and undramatic setting of socialist Britain. The untheatricality of most British Socialist leaders is a mark of uprightness and intellectual integrity, but it handicaps the experiment of nationalization which is undoubtedly the central purpose of their lives.[1]

The indispensability of play-acting in the grim business of dying and killing is particularly evident in the case of armies. Their uniforms, flags, emblems, parades, music, and elaborate etiquette and ritual are designed to separate the soldier from his flesh-and-blood self and mask the overwhelming reality of life and death. We speak of the theater of war and of battle scenes. In their battle orders army leaders invariably remind their soldiers that the eyes of the world are on them, that their ancestors are watching them and that posterity shall hear of them. The great general knows how to conjure an audience out of the sands of the desert and the waves of the ocean.

Glory is largely a theatrical concept. There is no striving for glory without a vivid awareness of an audience—the knowledge that our mighty deeds will come to the ears of our contemporaries or "of those who are to be." We are ready to sacrifice our true, transitory self for the imaginary eternal self we are building up, by our heroic deeds, in the opinion and imagination of others.

In the practice of mass movements, make-believe plays perhaps a more enduring role than any other factor. When faith and the power to persuade or coerce are gone, make-believe lingers on. There is no doubt that in staging its processions, parades, rituals and ceremonials, a mass movement touches a responsive chord in every heart. Even the most sober-minded are carried away by the sight of an impressive mass spectacle. There is an exhilaration and getting out of one's skin in both participants and spectators. It is possible that the frustrated are more responsive to the might and splendor of the mass than people who are self-sufficient. The desire to escape or camouflage their unsatisfactory selves develops in the frustrated a facility for pretending—for making a show—and also a readiness to identify themselves wholly with an imposing mass spectacle.

DEPRECATION OF THE PRESENT

48

At its inception a mass movement seems to champion the present against the past. It sees in the established institutions and privileges an encroachment of a senile, vile past on a virginal present. But, to pry loose the stranglehold of the past, there is need for utmost unity and unlimited self-sacrifice. This means that the people called upon to attack the past in order to liberate the present must be willing to give up enthusiastically any chance of ever tasting or inheriting the present. The absurdity of the proposition is obvious. Hence the inevitable shift in emphasis once the movement starts rolling. The present—the original objective—is shoved off the stage and its place taken by posterity—the future. More still: the present is driven back as if it were an unclean thing and lumped with the detested past. The battle line is now drawn between things that are and have been, and the things that are not yet.

To lose one's life is but to lose the present; and, clearly, to lose a defiled, worthless present is not to lose much.

Not only does a mass movement depict the present as mean and miserable—it deliberately makes it so. It fashions a pattern of individual existence that is dour, hard, repressive and dull. It decries pleasures and comforts and extols the rigorous life. It views ordinary enjoyment as trivial or even discreditable, and represents the pursuit of personal happiness as immoral. To enjoy oneself is to have truck with the enemy—the present. The prime objective of the ascetic ideal preached by most movements is to breed contempt for the present. The campaign against the appetites is an effort to pry loose tenacious tentacles holding on to the present. That this cheerless individual life runs its course against a colorful and dramatic background of collective pageantry serves to accentuate its worthlessness.

The very impracticability of many of the goals which a mass movement sets itself is part of the campaign against the present. All that is practicable, feasible and possible

is part of the present. To offer something practicable
would be to increase the promise of the present and reconcile us with it. Faith in miracles, too, implies a rejection
and a defiance of the present. When Tertullian proclaimed, "And He was buried and rose again; it is certain
because it is impossible," he was snapping his fingers at
the present. Finally, the mysticism of a movement is also
a means of deprecating the present. It sees the present as
the faded and distorted reflection of a vast unknown
throbbing underneath and beyond us. The present is a
shadow and an illusion.

49

There can be no genuine deprecation of the present without the assured hope of a better future. For however much
we lament the baseness of our times, if the prospect offered by the future is that of advanced deterioration or
even an unchanged continuation of the present, we are
inevitably moved to reconcile ourselves with our existence—difficult and mean though it may be.

All mass movements deprecate the present by depicting
it as a mean preliminary to a glorious future; a mere door-
mat on the threshold of the millennium. To a religious
movement the present is a place of exile, a vale of tears
leading to the heavenly kingdom; to a social revolution it
is a mean way station on the road to Utopia; to a nationalist movement it is an ignoble episode preceding the final
triumph.

It is true of course that the hope released by a vivid
visualization of a glorious future is a most potent source
of daring and self-forgetting—more potent than the implied deprecation of the present. A mass movement has to
center the hearts and minds of its followers on the future
even when it is not engaged in a life-and-death struggle

with established institutions and privileges. The self-sacrifice involved in mutual sharing and co-operative action is impossible without hope. When today is all there is, we grab all we can and hold on. We are afloat in an ocean of nothingness and we hang on to any miserable piece of wreckage as if it were the tree of life. On the other hand, when everything is ahead and yet to come, we find it easy to share all we have and to forego advantages within our grasp. The behavior of the members of the Donner party when they were buoyed by hope and, later, when hope was gone illustrates the dependence of co-operativeness and the communal spirit on hope. Those without hope are divided and driven to desperate self-seeking. Common suffering by itself, when not joined with hope, does not unite nor does it evoke mutual generosity. The enslaved Hebrews in Egypt, "their lives made bitter with hard bondage," were a bickering, back-biting lot. Moses had to give them hope of a promised land before he could join them together. The thirty thousand hopeless people in the concentration camp of Buchenwald did not develop any form of united action, nor did they manifest any readiness for self-sacrifice. There was more greed and ruthless selfishness there than in the greediest and most corrupt of free societies. "Instead of studying the way in which they could best help each other they used all their ingenuity to dominate and oppress each other."[2]

50

A glorification of the past can serve as a means to belittle the present. But unless joined with sanguine expectations of the future, an exaggerated view of the past results in an attitude of caution and not in the reckless strivings of a mass movement. On the other hand, there is no more potent dwarfing of the present than by viewing it as a mere link between a glorious past and a glorious future. Thus, though a mass movement at first turns its back on the past, it eventually develops a vivid awareness, often specious, of a distant glorious past. Religious movements go back to the day of creation; social revolutions tell of a golden age when men were free, equal and independent; nationalist movements revive or invent memories of past greatness. This preoccupation with the past stems not only from a desire to demonstrate the legitimacy of the movement and the illegitimacy of the old order, but also to show up the present as a mere interlude between past and future.[3]

An historical awareness also imparts a sense of continuity. Possessed of a vivid vision of past and future, the true believer sees himself part of something that stretches endlessly backward and forward—something eternal. He can let go of the present (and of his own life) not only because it is a poor thing, hardly worth hanging on to, but also because it is not the beginning and the end of all things. Furthermore, a vivid awareness of past and future robs the present of its reality. It makes the present seem as a section in a procession or a parade. The followers of a mass movement see themselves on the march with drums beating and colors flying. They are participators in a soul-stirring drama played to a vast audience—generations gone and generations yet to come. They are made to feel that they are not their real selves but actors playing a role, and their doings a "performance," rather than as the real thing. Dying, too, they see as a gesture, an act of make-believe.

51

A deprecating attitude toward the present fosters a capacity for prognostication. The well-adjusted make poor prophets. On the other hand, those who are at war with the present have an eye for the seeds of change and the potentialities of small beginnings.

A pleasant existence blinds us to the possibilities of drastic change. We cling to what we call our common sense, our practical point of view. Actually, these are but names for an all-absorbing familiarity with things as they are. The tangibility of a pleasant and secure existence is such that it makes other realities, however imminent, seem vague and visionary. Thus it happens that when the times become unhinged, it is the practical people who are caught unaware and are made to look like visionaries who cling to things that do not exist.

On the other hand, those who reject the present and fix their eyes and hearts on things to come have a faculty for detecting the embryo of future danger or advantage in the ripeness of their times. Hence the frustrated individual and the true believer make better prognosticators than those who have reason to want the preservation of the status quo. "It is often the fanatics, and not always the delicate spirits, that are found grasping the right thread of the solutions required by the future."[4]

52

It is of interest to compare here the attitudes toward present, future and past shown by the conservative, the liberal, the skeptic, the radical and the reactionary.

The conservative doubts that the present can be bettered, and he tries to shape the future in the image of the present. He goes to the past for reassurance about the present: "I wanted the sense of continuity, the assurance that our contemporary blunders were endemic in human nature, that our new fads were very ancient heresies, that beloved things which were threatened had rocked not less heavily in the past."[5] How, indeed, like the skeptic is the conservative! "Is there any thing whereof it may be said, See this is new? it hath been already of old time, which was before us."[6] To the skeptic the present is the sum of all that has been and shall be. "The thing that hath been, it is that which shall be; and that which is done is that which shall be done: and there is no new thing under the sun."[7] The liberal sees the present as the legitimate off-spring of the past and as constantly growing and developing toward an improved future: to damage the present is to maim the future. All three then cherish the present, and, as one would expect, they do not take willingly to the idea of self-sacrifice. Their attitude toward self-sacrifice is best expressed by the skeptic: "for a living dog is better than a dead lion. For the living know that they shall die: but the dead know not any thing . . . neither have they any more a portion for ever in any thing that is done under the sun."[8]

The radical and the reactionary loathe the present. They see it as an aberration and a deformity. Both are ready to proceed ruthlessly and recklessly with the present, and both are hospitable to the idea of self-sacrifice. Wherein do they differ? Primarily in their view of the malleability of man's nature. The radical has a passionate faith in the infinite perfectibility of human nature. He believes that by changing man's environment and by perfecting a technique of soul forming, a society can be wrought that is wholly new and unprecedented. The reactionary does not believe that man has unfathomed potentialities for good in him. If a stable and healthy society is to be established, it must be patterned after the proven models of the past. He sees the future as a glorious restoration rather than an unprecedented innovation.

In reality the boundary line between radical and reactionary is not always distinct. The reactionary manifests radicalism when he comes to recreate his ideal past. His image of the past is based less on what it actually was than on what he wants the future to be. He innovates more than he reconstructs. A somewhat similar shift occurs in the case of the radical when he goes about building his new world. He feels the need for practical guidance, and since he has rejected and destroyed the present he is compelled to link the new world with some point in the past. If he has to employ violence in shaping the new, his view of man's nature darkens and approaches closer to that of the reactionary.

The blending of the reactionary and the radical is particularly evident in those engaged in a nationalist revival. The followers of Gandhi in India and the Zionists in Palestine would revive a glorified past and simultaneously create an unprecedented Utopia. The prophets, too, were a blend of the reactionary and the radical. They preached a return to the ancient faith and also envisaged a new world and a new life.

53

That the deprecating attitude of a mass movement toward the present seconds the inclinations of the frustrated is obvious. What surprises one, when listening to the frustrated as they decry the present and all its works, is the enormous joy they derive from doing so. Such delight cannot come from the mere venting of a grievance. There must be something more—and there is. By expatiating upon the incurable baseness and vileness of the times, the frustrated soften their feeling of failure and isolation. It is as if they said: "Not only our blemished selves, but the lives of all our contemporaries, even the most happy and successful, are worthless and wasted." Thus by deprecating the present they acquire a vague sense of equality.

The means, also, a mass movement uses to make the

present unpalatable (Section 48) strike a responsive chord in the frustrated. The self-mastery needed in overcoming their appetites gives them an illusion of strength. They feel that in mastering themselves they have mastered the world. The mass movement's advocacy of the impracticable and impossible also agrees with their taste. Those who fail in everyday affairs show a tendency to reach out for the impossible. It is a device to camouflage their shortcomings. For when we fail in attempting the possible, the blame is solely ours; but when we fail in attempting the impossible, we are justified in attributing it to the magnitude of the task. There is less risk in being discredited when trying the impossible than when trying the possible. It is thus that failure in everyday affairs often breeds an extravagant audacity.

One gains the impression that the frustrated derive as much satisfaction—if not more—from the means a mass movement uses as from the ends it advocates. The delight of the frustrated in chaos and in the downfall of the fortunate and prosperous does not spring from an ecstatic awareness that they are clearing the ground for the heavenly city. In their fanatical cry of "all or nothing at all" the second alternative echoes perhaps a more ardent wish than the first.

"THINGS WHICH ARE NOT"

54

One of the rules that emerges from a consideration of the factors that promote self-sacrifice is that we are less ready to die for what we have or are than for what we wish to have and to be. It is a perplexing and unpleasant truth that when men already have "something worth fighting for," they do not feel like fighting. People who live full, worthwhile lives are not usually ready to die for their own interests nor for their country nor for a holy cause.[9] Craving, not having, is the mother of a reckless giving of oneself.

"Things which are not" are indeed mightier than "things that are."[10] In all ages men have fought most desperately for beautiful cities yet to be built and gardens yet to be planted. Satan did not digress to tell all he knew when he said: "All that a man hath will he give for his life."[11] All he hath—yes. But he sooner dies than yield aught of that which he hath not yet.

It is strange, indeed, that those who hug the present and hang on to it with all their might should be the least capable of defending it. And that, on the other hand, those who spurn the present and dust their hands of it should have all its gifts and treasures showered on them unasked.

Dreams, visions and wild hopes are mighty weapons and realistic tools. The practical-mindedness of a true leader consists in recognizing the practical value of these tools. Yet this recognition usually stems from a contempt of the present which can be traced to a natural ineptitude in practical affairs. The successful businessman is often a failure as a communal leader because his mind is attuned to the "things that are" and his heart set on that which can be accomplished in "our time." Failure in the management of practical affairs seems to be a qualification for success in the management of public affairs. And it is perhaps fortunate that some proud natures when suffering defeat in the practical world do not feel crushed but are suddenly fired with the apparently absurd conviction that they are eminently competent to direct the fortunes of the community and the nation.

55

It is not altogether absurd that people should be ready to die for a button, a flag, a word, an opinion, a myth and so on. It is on the contrary the least reasonable thing to give one's life for something palpably worth having. For, surely, one's life is the most real of all things real, and without it there can be no having of things worth having. Self-sacrifice cannot be a manifestation of tangible self-interest. Even when we are ready to die in order not to get killed, the impulse to fight springs less from self-interest than from intangibles such as tradition, honor (a word), and, above all, hope. Where there is no hope, people either run, or allow themselves to be killed without a fight. They will hang on to life as in a daze. How else explain the fact that millions of Europeans allowed themselves to be led into annihilation camps and gas chambers, knowing beyond doubt that they were being led to death? It was not the least of Hitler's formidable powers that he knew how to drain his opponents (at least in continental Europe) of all hope. His fanatical conviction that he was building a new order that would last a thousand years communicated itself both to followers and antagonists. To the former it gave the feeling that in fighting for the Third Reich they were in league with eternity, while the latter felt that to struggle against Hitler's new order was to defy inexorable fate.

It is of interest that the Jews who submitted to extermination in Hitler's Europe fought recklessly when transferred to Palestine. And though it is said that they fought in Palestine because they had no choice—they had to fight or have their throats cut by the Arabs—it is still true that their daring and reckless readiness for self-sacrifice sprang not from despair but from their fervent preoccupation with the revival of an ancient land and an ancient people. They, indeed, fought and died for cities yet to be built and gardens yet to be planted.

DOCTRINE

56

The readiness for self-sacrifice is contingent on an imperviousness to the realities of life. He who is free to draw conclusions from his individual experience and observation is not usually hospitable to the idea of martyrdom. For self-sacrifice is an unreasonable act. It cannot be the end-product of a process of probing and deliberating. All active mass movements strive, therefore, to interpose a fact-proof screen between the faithful and the realities of the world. They do this by claiming that the ultimate and absolute truth is already embodied in their doctrine and that there is no truth nor certitude outside it. The facts on which the true believer bases his conclusions must not be derived from his experience or observation but from holy writ. "So tenaciously should we cling to the world revealed by the Gospel, that were I to see all the Angels of Heaven coming down to me to tell me something different, not only would I not be tempted to doubt a single syllable, but I would shut my eyes and stop my ears, for they would not deserve to be either seen or heard."[12] To rely on the evidence of the senses and of reason is heresy and treason. It is startling to realize how much unbelief is necessary to make belief possible. What we know as blind faith is sustained by innumerable unbeliefs. The fanatical Japanese in Brazil refused to believe for years the evidence of Japan's defeat. The fanatical Communist refuses to believe any unfavorable report or evidence about Russia, nor will he be disillusioned by seeing with his own eyes the cruel misery inside the Soviet promised land.

It is the true believer's ability to "shut his eyes and stop his ears" to facts that do not deserve to be either seen or heard which is the source of his unequaled fortitude and constancy. He cannot be frightened by danger nor disheartened by obstacles nor baffled by contradictions because he denies their existence. Strength of faith, as Bergson pointed out, manifests itself not in moving mountains but in not seeing mountains to move.[13] And it is the certitude of his infallible doctrine that renders the true believer impervious to the uncertainties, surprises and the unpleasant realities of the world around him.

Thus the effectiveness of a doctrine should not be judged by its profundity, sublimity or the validity of the truths it embodies, but by how thoroughly it insulates the individual from his self and the world as it is. What Pascal said of an effective religion is true of any effective doctrine: it must be "contrary to nature, to common sense and to pleasure."[14]

57

The effectiveness of a doctrine does not come from its meaning but from its certitude. No doctrine however profound and sublime will be effective unless it is presented as the embodiment of the one and only truth. It must be the one word from which all things are and all things speak.[15] Crude absurdities, trivial nonsense and sublime truths are equally potent in readying people for self-sacrifice if they are accepted as the sole, eternal truth.

It is obvious, therefore, that in order to be effective a doctrine must not be understood, but has rather to be believed in. We can be absolutely certain only about things we do not understand. A doctrine that is understood is shorn of its strength. Once we understand a thing, it is as if it had originated in us. And, clearly, those who are asked to renounce the self and sacrifice it cannot see eternal certitude in anything which originates in that self. The fact that they understand a thing fully impairs its validity and certitude in their eyes.

The devout are always urged to seek the absolute truth with their hearts and not their minds. "It is the heart which is conscious of God, not the reason."[16] Rudolph Hess, when swearing in the entire Nazi party in 1934, exhorted his hearers: "Do not seek Adolph Hitler with your brains; all of you will find him with the strength of your hearts."[17] When a movement begins to rationalize its doctrine and make it intelligible, it is a sign that its dynamic span is over; that it is primarily interested in stability. For, as will be shown later (Section 106), the stability of a regime requires the allegiance of the intellectuals, and it is to win them rather than to foster self-sacrifice in the masses that a doctrine is made intelligible.

If a doctrine is not unintelligible, it has to be vague; and if neither unintelligible nor vague, it has to be unverifiable. One has to get to heaven or the distant future to determine the truth of an effective doctrine. When some part of a doctrine is relatively simple, there is a tendency among the faithful to complicate and obscure it. Simple words are made pregnant with meaning and made to look like symbols in a secret message. There is thus an illiterate air about the most literate true believer. He seems to use words as if he were ignorant of their true meaning. Hence, too, his taste for quibbling, hair-splitting and scholastic tortuousness.

58

To be in possession of an absolute truth is to have a net of familiarity spread over the whole of eternity. There are no surprises and no unknowns. All questions have already been answered, all decisions made, all eventualities foreseen. The true believer is without wonder and hesitation. "Who knows Jesus knows the reason of all things."[18] The true doctrine is a master key to all the world's problems. With it the world can be taken apart and put together. The official history of the Communist party states: "The power of Marxist-Leninist theory lies in the fact that it enables the Party to find the right orientation in any situation, to understand the inner connection of current events, to foresee their course, and to perceive not only how and in what direction they are developing in the present but how and in what direction they are bound to develop in the future."[19] The true believer is emboldened to attempt the unprecedented and the impossible not only because his doctrine gives him a sense of omnipotence but also because it gives him unqualified confidence in the future. (See Section 4.)

An active mass movement rejects the present and centers its interest on the future. It is from this attitude that it derives its strength, for it can proceed recklessly with the present—with the health, wealth and lives of its followers. But it must act as if had already read the book of the future to the last word. Its doctrine is proclaimed as a key to that book.

59

Are the frustrated more easily indoctrinated than the non-frustrated? Are they more credulous? Pascal was of the opinion that "one was well-minded to understand holy writ when one hated oneself."[20] There is apparently some connection between dissatisfaction with oneself and a proneness to credulity. The urge to escape our real self is also an urge to escape the rational and the obvious. The refusal to see ourselves as we are develops a distaste for facts and cold logic. There is no hope for the frustrated in the actual and the possible. Salvation can come to them only from the miraculous, which seeps through a crack in the iron wall of inexorable reality. They ask to be deceived. What Stresemann said of the Germans is true of the frustrated in general: "[They] pray not only for [their] daily bread, but also for [their] daily illusion."[21] The rule seems to be that those who find no difficulty in deceiving themselves are easily deceived by others. They are easily persuaded and led.

A peculiar side of credulity is that it is often joined with a proneness to imposture. The association of believing and lying is not characteristic solely of children. The inability or unwillingness to see things as they are promotes both gullibility and charlatanism.

FANATICISM

60

It was suggested in Section 1 that mass movements are often necessary for the realization of drastic and abrupt changes. It seems strange that even practical and desirable changes, such as the renovation of stagnant societies, should require for their realization an atmosphere of intense passion and should have to be accompanied by all the faults and follies of an active mass movement. The surprise lessens when we realize that the chief preoccupation of an active mass movement is to instill in its followers a facility for united action and self-sacrifice, and that it achieves this facility by stripping each human entity of its distinctness and autonomy and turning it into an anonymous particle with no will and no judgment of its own. The result is not only a compact and fearless following but also a homogeneous plastic mass that can be kneaded at will. The human plasticity necessary for the realization of drastic and abrupt changes seems, therefore, to be a by-product of the process of unification and of the inculcation of a readiness for self-sacrifice.

The important point is that the estrangement from the self, which is a precondition for both plasticity and conversion, almost always proceeds in an atmosphere of intense passion. For not only is the stirring of passion an effective means of upsetting an established equilibrium between a man and his self, but it is also the inevitable by-product of such an upsetting. Passion is released even when the estrangement from the self is brought about by the most unemotional means. Only the individual who has come to terms with his self can have a dispassionate attitude toward the world. Once the harmony with the self is upset, and a man is impelled to reject, renounce, distrust or forget his self, he turns into a highly reactive entity. Like an unstable chemical radical he hungers to combine with whatever comes within his reach. He cannot stand apart, poised and self-sufficient, but has to attach himself wholeheartedly to one side or another.

By kindling and fanning violent passions in the hearts of their followers, mass movements prevent the settling of an inner balance. They also employ direct means to effect an enduring estrangement from the self. They depict an autonomous, self-sufficient existence not only as barren and meaningless but also as depraved and evil. Man on his own is a helpless, miserable and sinful creature. His only salvation is in rejecting his self and in finding a new life in the bosom of a holy corporate body—be it a church, a nation or a party. In its turn, this vilification of the self keeps passion at a white heat.

61

The fanatic is perpetually incomplete and insecure. He cannot generate self-assurance out of his individual resources—out of his rejected self—but finds it only by clinging passionately to whatever support he happens to embrace. This passionate attachment is the essence of his blind devotion and religiosity, and he sees in it the source of all virtue and strength. Though his single-minded dedication is a holding on for dear life, he easily sees himself as the supporter and defender of the holy cause to which he clings. And he is ready to sacrifice his life to demonstrate to himself and others that such indeed is his role. He sacrifices his life to prove his worth.

It goes without saying that the fanatic is convinced that the cause he holds on to is monolithic and eternal—a rock of ages. Still, his sense of security is derived from his passionate attachment and not from the excellence of his cause. The fanatic is not really a stickler to principle. He embraces a cause not primarily because of its justness and holiness but because of his desperate need for something to hold on to. Often, indeed, it is his need for passionate attachment which turns every cause he embraces into a holy cause.

The fanatic cannot be weaned away from his cause by an appeal to his reason or moral sense. He fears compromise and cannot be persuaded to qualify the certitude and righteousness of his holy cause. But he finds no difficulty in swinging suddenly and wildly from one holy cause to another. He cannot be convinced but only converted. His passionate attachment is more vital than the quality of the cause to which he is attached.

62

Though they seem to be at opposite poles, fanatics of all kinds are actually crowded together at one end. It is the fanatic and the moderate who are poles apart and never meet. The fanatics of various hues eye each other with suspicion and are ready to fly at each other's throat. But they are neighbors and almost of one family. They hate each other with the hatred of brothers. They are as far apart and close together as Saul and Paul. And it is easier for a fanatic Communist to be converted to fascism, chauvinism or Catholicism than to become a sober liberal.[22]

The opposite of the religious fanatic is not the fanatical atheist but the gentle cynic who cares not whether there is a God or not. The atheist is a religious person. He believes in atheism as though it were a new religion.[23] He is an atheist with devoutness and unction. According to Renan, "The day after that on which the world should no longer believe in God, atheists would be the wretchedest of all men."[24] So, too, the opposite of the chauvinist is not the traitor but the reasonable citizen who is in love with the present and has no taste for martyrdom and the heroic gesture. The traitor is usually a fanatic—radical or reactionary—who goes over to the enemy in order to hasten the downfall of a world he loathes. Most of the traitors in the Second World War came from the extreme right. "There seems to be a thin line between violent, extreme nationalism and treason."[25]

The kinship between the reactionary and the radical has been dealt with in Section 52. All of us who lived through the Hitler decade know that the reactionary and the radical have more in common than either has with the liberal or the conservative.

63

It is doubtful whether the fanatic who deserts his holy cause or is suddenly left without one can ever adjust himself to an autonomous individual existence. He remains a homeless hitch-hiker on the highways of the world thumbing a ride on any eternal cause that rolls by. An individual existence, even when purposeful, seems to him trivial, futile and sinful. To live without an ardent dedication is to be adrift and abandoned. He sees in tolerance a sign of weakness, frivolity and ignorance. He hungers for the deep assurance which comes with total surrender—with the wholehearted clinging to a creed and a cause. What matters is not the contents of the cause but the total dedication and the communion with a congregation. He is even ready to join in a holy crusade against his former holy cause, but it must be a genuine crusade—uncompromising, intolerant, proclaiming the one and only truth.

Thus the millions of ex-fanatics in defeated Germany and Japan are more responsive to the preaching of communism and militant Catholicism than to the teaching of the democratic way of life. The greater success of Communist propaganda in this case is not due to its superior technique but to the peculiar bias of the once fanatical Germans and Japanese. The spokesmen of democracy offer no holy cause to cling to and no corporate whole to lose oneself in. Communist Russia can easily turn Japanese war prisoners into fanatical Communists, while no American propaganda, however subtle and perfect, can turn them into freedom-loving democrats.

MASS MOVEMENTS AND ARMIES

64

It is well at this point, before leaving the subject of self-sacrifice, to have a look at the similarities and differences between mass movements and armies—a problem which has already cropped up in Sections 35 and 47.

The similarities are many: both mass movements and armies are collective bodies; both strip the individual of his separateness and distinctness; both demand self-sacrifice, unquestioning obedience and singlehearted allegiance; both make extensive use of make-belief to promote daring and united action (see Section 47); and both can serve as a refuge for the frustrated who cannot endure an autonomous existence. A military body like the Foreign Legion attracts many of the types who usually rush to join a new movement. It is also true that the recruiting officer, the Communist agitator and the missionary often fish simultaneously in the cesspools of Skid Row.

But the differences are fundamental: an army does not come to fulfill a need for a new way of life; it is not a road to salvation. It can be used as a stick in the hand of a coercer to impose a new way of life and force it down unwilling throats. But the army is mainly an instrument devised for the preservation or expansion of an established order—old or new. It is a temporary instrument that can be assembled and taken apart at will. The mass movement, on the other hand, seems an instrument of eternity, and those who join it do so for life. The ex-soldier is a veteran, even a hero; the ex–true believer is a renegade. The army is an instrument for bolstering, protecting and expanding the present. The mass movement comes to destroy the present. Its preoccupation is with the future, and it derives its vigor and drive from this preoccupation.

When a mass movement begins to be preoccupied with the present, it means that it has arrived. It ceases then to be a movement and becomes an institutionalized organization—an established church, a government or an army (of soldiers or workers). The popular army, which is often an end-product of a mass movement, retains many of the trappings of the movement—pious verbiage, slogans, holy symbols; but like any other army it is held together less by faith and enthusiasm than by the unimpassioned mechanism of drill, esprit de corps and coercion. It soon loses the asceticism and unction of a holy congregation and displays the boisterousness and the taste for the joys of the present which is characteristic of all armies.

Being an instrument of the present, an army deals mainly with the possible. Its leaders do not rely on miracles. Even when animated by fervent faith, they are open to compromise. They reckon with the possibility of defeat and know how to surrender. On the other hand, the leader of a mass movement has an overwhelming contempt for the present—for all its stubborn facts and perplexities, even those of geography and the weather. He relies on miracles. His hatred of the present (his nihilism) comes to the fore when the situation becomes desperate. He destroys his country and his people rather than surrender.

The spirit of self-sacrifice within an army is fostered by devotion to duty, make-believe, esprit de corps, drill, faith in a leader, sportsmanship, the spirit of adventure and the desire for glory. These factors, unlike those employed by a mass movement, do not spring from a deprecation of the present and a revulsion from an unwanted self. They can unfold therefore in a sober atmosphere. The fanatical soldier is usually a fanatic turned soldier rather than the other way around. An army's spirit of self-sacrifice is most nobly expressed in the words Sarpedon spoke to Glaucus as they stormed the Grecian wall: "O my friend, if we, leaving this war, could escape from age and death, I should not here be fighting in the van; but now, since many are the modes of death impending over us which no man can hope to shun, let us press on and give renown to other men, or win it for ourselves."[26]

The most striking difference between mass movements and armies is in their attitude to the multitude and the rabble. De Tocqueville observes that soldiers are "the men who lose their heads most easily, and who generally show themselves weakest on days of revolution."[27] To the typical general the mass is something his army would turn into if it were to fall apart. He is more aware of the inconstancy of the mass and its will to anarchy than of its readiness for self-sacrifice. He sees it as the poisonous end-product of a crumbling collective body rather than the raw material of a new world. His attitude is a mixture of fear and contempt. He knows how to suppress the mass but not how to win it. On the other hand, the mass movement leader—from Moses to Hitler—draws his inspiration from the sea of upturned faces, and the roar of the mass is as the voice of God in his ears. He sees an irresistible force within his reach—a force he alone can harness. And with this force he will sweep away empires and armies and all the mighty present. The face of the mass is as "the face of the deep" out of which, like God on the day of creation, he will bring forth a new world.

XIV

Unifying Agents

HATRED

65

Hatred is the most accessible and comprehensive of all unifying agents. It pulls and whirls the individual away from his own self, makes him oblivious of his weal and future, frees him of jealousies and self-seeking. He becomes an anonymous particle quivering with a craving to fuse and coalesce with his like into one flaming mass. Heine suggests that what Christian love cannot do is effected by a common hatred.[1]

Mass movements can rise and spread without belief in a God, but never without belief in a devil. Usually the strength of a mass movement is proportionate to the vividness and tangibility of its devil. When Hitler was asked whether he thought the Jew must be destroyed, he answered: "No. . . . We should have then to invent him. It is essential to have a tangible enemy, not merely an abstract one."[2] F. A. Voigt tells of a Japanese mission that arrived in Berlin in 1932 to study the National Socialist movement. Voigt asked a member of the mission what he thought of the movement. He replied: "It is magnificent. I wish we could have something like it in Japan, only we can't, because we haven't got any Jews."[3] It is perhaps true that the insight and shrewdness of the men who know how to set a mass movement in motion, or how to keep one going, manifest themselves as much in knowing how to pick a worthy enemy as in knowing what doctrine to embrace and what program to adopt. The theoreticians of the Kremlin hardly waited for the guns of the Second World War to cool before they picked the democratic West, and particularly America, as the chosen enemy. It is doubtful whether any gesture of goodwill or any concession from our side will reduce the volume and venom of vilification against us emanating from the Kremlin.

One of Chiang Kai-shek's most serious shortcomings was his failure to find an appropriate new devil once the Japanese enemy vanished from the scene at the end of the war. The ambitious but simple-minded General was perhaps too conceited to realize that it was not he but the Japanese devil who generated the enthusiasm, the unity and the readiness for self-sacrifice of the Chinese masses.

66

Common hatred unites the most heterogeneous elements. To share a common hatred, with an enemy even, is to infect him with a feeling of kinship, and thus sap his powers of resistance. Hitler used anti-Semitism not only to unify his Germans but also to sap the resoluteness of Jew-hating Poland, Rumania, Hungary, and finally even France. He made a similar use of anti-communism.

67

It seems that, like the ideal deity, the ideal devil is one. We have it from Hitler—the foremost authority on devils—that the genius of a great leader consists in concentrating all hatred on a single foe, making "even adversaries far removed from one another seem to belong to a single category."[4] When Hitler picked the Jew as his devil, he peopled practically the whole world outside Germany with Jews or those who worked for them. "Behind England stands Israel, and behind France, and behind the United States."[5] Stalin, too, adheres to the monotheistic principle when picking a devil. Formerly this devil was a fascist; now he is an American plutocrat.

Again, like an ideal deity, the ideal devil is omnipotent and omnipresent. When Hitler was asked whether he was not attributing rather too much importance to the Jews, he exclaimed: "No, no, no! . . . It is impossible to exaggerate the formidable quality of the Jew as an enemy."[6] Every difficulty and failure within the movement is the work of the devil, and every success is a triumph over his evil plotting.[7]

Finally, it seems, the ideal devil is a foreigner. To qualify as a devil, a domestic enemy must be given a foreign ancestry. Hitler found it easy to brand the German Jews as foreigners. The Russian revolutionary agitators emphasized the foreign origin (Varangian, Tartar, Western) of the Russian aristocracy.[8] In the French Revolution the aristocrats were seen as "descendants of barbarous Germans, while French commoners were descendants of civilized Gauls and Romans."[9] In the Puritan Revolution the royalists "were labeled 'Normans,' descendants of a group of foreign invaders."[10]

68

We do not usually look for allies when we love. Indeed, we often look on those who love with us as rivals and trespassers. But we always look for allies when we hate.

It is understandable that we should look for others to side with us when we have a just grievance and crave to retaliate against those who wronged us. The puzzling thing is that when our hatred does not spring from a visible grievance and does not seem justified, the desire for allies becomes more pressing. It is chiefly the unreasonable hatreds that drive us to merge with those who hate as we do, and it is this kind of hatred that serves as one of the most effective cementing agents.

Whence come these unreasonable hatreds, and why their unifying effect? They are an expression of a desperate effort to suppress an awareness of our inadequacy, worthlessness, guilt and other shortcomings of the self. Self-contempt is here transmuted into hatred of others—and there is a most determined and persistent effort to mask this switch. Obviously, the most effective way of doing this is to find others, as many as possible, who hate as we do. Here more than anywhere else we need general consent, and much of our proselytizing consists perhaps in infecting others not with our brand of faith but with our particular brand of unreasonable hatred.

Even in the case of a just grievance, our hatred comes less from a wrong done to us than from the consciousness of our helplessness, inadequacy and cowardice—in other words from self-contempt. When we feel superior to our tormentors, we are likely to despise them, even pity them, but not hate them.[11] That the relation between grievance and hatred is not simple and direct is also seen from the fact that the released hatred is not always directed against those who wronged us. Often, when we are wronged by one person, we turn our hatred on a wholly unrelated person or group. Russians, bullied by Stalin's secret police, are easily inflamed against "capitalist warmongers"; Germans, aggrieved by the Versailles treaty, avenged themselves by exterminating Jews; Zulus, oppressed by Boers, butcher Hindus; white trash, exploited by Dixiecrats, lynch Blacks.

Self-contempt produces in man "the most unjust and

criminal passions imaginable, for he conceives a mortal hatred against that truth which blames him and convinces him of his faults."[12]

69

That hatred springs more from self-contempt than from a legitimate grievance is seen in the intimate connection between hatred and a guilty conscience.

There is perhaps no surer way of infecting ourselves with virulent hatred toward a person than by doing him a grave injustice. That others have a just grievance against us is a more potent reason for hating them than that we have a just grievance against them. We do not make people humble and meek when we show them their guilt and cause them to be ashamed of themselves. We are more likely to stir their arrogance and rouse in them a reckless aggressiveness. Self-righteousness is a loud din raised to drown the voice of guilt within us.

There is a guilty conscience behind every brazen word and act and behind every manifestation of self-righteousness.

70

To wrong those we hate is to add fuel to our hatred. Conversely, to treat an enemy with magnanimity is to blunt our hatred for him.

71

The most effective way to silence our guilty conscience is to convince ourselves and others that those we have sinned against are indeed depraved creatures, deserving every punishment, even extermination. We cannot pity those we have wronged, nor can we be indifferent toward them. We must hate and persecute them or else leave the door open to self-contempt.

72

A sublime religion inevitably generates a strong feeling of guilt. There is an unavoidable contrast between loftiness of profession and imperfection of practice. And, as one would expect, the feeling of guilt promotes hate and brazenness. Thus it seems that the more sublime the faith the more virulent the hatred it breeds.

73

It is easier to hate an enemy with much good in him than one who is all bad. We cannot hate those we despise. The Japanese had an advantage over us in that they admired us more than we admired them. They could hate us more fervently than we could hate them. The Americans are poor haters in international affairs because of their innate feeling of superiority over all foreigners. An American's hatred for a fellow American (for Hoover or Roosevelt) is far more virulent than any antipathy he can work up against foreigners. It is of interest that the backward South shows more xenophobia than the rest of the country. Should Americans begin to hate foreigners wholeheartedly, it will be an indication that they have lost confidence in their own way of life.

The undercurrent of admiration in hatred manifests itself in the inclination to imitate those we hate. Thus every mass movement shapes itself after its specific devil. Christianity at its height realized the image of the antichrist. The Jacobins practiced all the evils of the tyranny they had risen against. Soviet Russia is realizing the purest and most colossal example of monopolistic capitalism. Hitler took the Protocols of the Wise Men of Zion for his guide and textbook; he followed them "down to the veriest detail."[13]

It is startling to see how the oppressed almost invariably shape themselves in the image of their hated oppressors. That the evil men do lives after them is partly due to the fact that those who have reason to hate the evil most shape themselves after it and thus perpetuate it. It is obvious, therefore, that the influence of the fanatic is bound to be out of all proportion to his abilities. Both by converting and antagonizing, he shapes the world in his own image. Fanatic Christianity puts its imprint upon the ancient world both by gaining adherents and by evoking in its pagan opponents a strange fervor and a new ruthlessness. Hitler imposed himself upon the world both by promoting Nazism and by forcing the democracies to become zealous, intolerant and ruthless. Communist Russia shapes both its adherents and its opponents in its own image.

Thus, though hatred is a convenient instrument for mobilizing a community for defense, it does not, in the long run, come cheap. We pay for it by losing all or many of the values we have set out to defend.

Hitler, who sensed the undercurrent of admiration in hatred, drew a remarkable conclusion. It is of the utmost importance, he said, that the National Socialist should seek and deserve the violent hatred of his enemies. Such hatred would be proof of the superiority of the National Socialist faith. "The best yardstick for the value of his [the National Socialist's] attitude, for the sincerity of his conviction, and the force of his will is the hostility he receives from the . . . enemy."[14]

74

It seems that when we are oppressed by the knowledge of our worthlessness we do not see ourselves as lower than some and higher than others, but as lower than the lowest of mankind. We hate then the whole world, and we would pour our wrath upon the whole of creation.

There is a deep reassurance for the frustrated in witnessing the downfall of the fortunate and the disgrace of the righteous. They see in a general downfall an approach to the brotherhood of all. Chaos, like the grave, is a haven of equality. Their burning conviction that there must be a new life and a new order is fueled by the realization that the old will have to be razed to the ground before the new can be built. Their clamor for a millennium is shot through with a hatred for all that exists, and a craving for the end of the world.

75

Passionate hatred can give meaning and purpose to an empty life. Thus people haunted by the purposelessness of their lives try to find a new content not only by dedicating themselves to a holy cause but also by nursing a fanatical grievance. A mass movement offers them unlimited opportunities for both.

76

Whether it is true or not as Pascal says that "all men by nature hate each other," and that love and charity are only "a feint and a false image, for at bottom they are but hate,"[15] one cannot escape the impression that hatred is an all-pervading ingredient in the compounds and combinations of our inner life. All our enthusiasms, devotions, passions and hopes, when they decompose, release hatred. On the other hand it is possible to synthesize an enthusiasm, a devotion and a hope by activating hatred. Said Martin Luther: "When my heart is cold and I cannot pray as I should I scourge myself with the thought of the impiety and ingratitude of my enemies, the Pope and his accomplices and vermin, and Zwingli, so that my heart swells with righteous indignation and hatred and I can say with warmth and vehemence: 'Holy be Thy Name, Thy Kingdom come, Thy Will be done!' And the hotter I grow the more ardent do my prayers become."[16]

77

Unity and self-sacrifice, of themselves, even when fostered by the most noble means, produce a facility for hating. Even when men league themselves mightily together to promote tolerance and peace on earth, they are likely to be violently intolerant toward those not of a like mind.

The estrangement from the self, without which there can be neither selflessness nor a full assimilation of the individual into a compact whole, produces, as already mentioned,[17] a proclivity for passionate attitudes, including passionate hatred. There are also other factors which favor the growth of hatred in an atmosphere of unity and selflessness. The act of self-denial seems to confer on us the right to be harsh and merciless toward others. The impression somehow prevails that the true believer, particularly the religious individual, is a humble person. The truth is that the surrendering and humbling of the self breed pride and arrogance. The true believer is apt to see himself as one of the chosen, the salt of the earth, the light of the world, a prince disguised in meekness, who is destined to inherit this earth and the kingdom of heaven, too.[18] He who is not of his faith is evil; he who will not listen shall perish.

There is also this: when we renounce the self and become part of a compact whole, we not only renounce personal advantage but are also rid of personal responsibility. There is no telling to what extremes of cruelty and ruthlessness a man will go when he is freed from the fears, hesitations, doubts and the vague stirrings of decency that go with individual judgment. When we lose our individual independence in the corporateness of a mass movement, we find a new freedom—freedom to hate, bully, lie, torture, murder and betray without shame and remorse. Herein undoubtedly lies part of the attractiveness of a mass movement. We find there the "right to dishonour," which according to Dostoyevsky has an irresistible fascination.[19] Hitler had a contemptuous opinion of the brutality of the autonomous individual. "Any violence which does not spring from a firm, spiritual base, will be wavering and uncertain. It lacks the stability which can only rest in a fanatical outlook."[20]

Thus hatred is not only a means of unification but also its product. Renan says that we have never, since the world began, heard of a merciful nation.[21] Nor, one may add, have we heard of a merciful church or a merciful revolutionary party. The hatred and cruelty which have their source in selfishness are ineffectual things compared with the venom and ruthlessness born of selflessness.

When we see the bloodshed, terror and destruction born of such generous enthusiasms as the love of God, love of Christ, love of a nation, compassion for the oppressed and so on, we usually blame this shameful perversion on a cynical, power-hungry leadership. Actually, it is the unification set in motion by these enthusiasms, rather than the manipulations of a scheming leadership, that transmutes noble impulses into a reality of hatred and violence. The deindividualization which is a prerequisite for thorough integration and selfless dedication is also, to a considerable extent, a process of dehumanization. The torture chamber is a corporate institution.

IMITATION

78

Imitation is an essential unifying agent. The development of a close-knit group is inconceivable without a diffusion of uniformity. The one-mindedness and *Gleichschaltung* prized by every mass movement are achieved as much by imitation as by obedience. Obedience itself consists as much in the imitation of an example as in the following of a precept.

Though the imitative capacity is present in all people, it can be stronger in some than in others. The question is whether the frustrated, who, as suggested in Section 43, not only have a propensity for united action but are also equipped with a mechanism for its realization, are particularly imitative. Is there a connection between frustration and the readiness to imitate? Is imitation in some manner a means of escape from the ills that beset the frustrated?

The chief burden of the frustrated is the consciousness of a blemished, ineffectual self, and their chief desire is to slough off the unwanted self and begin a new life. They try to realize this desire either by finding a new identity or by blurring and camouflaging their individual distinctness; and both these ends are reached by imitation.

The less satisfaction we derive from being ourselves, the greater is our desire to be like others. We are therefore more ready to imitate those who are different from us than those nearly like us, and those we admire than those we despise. The imitativeness of the oppressed (Blacks and Jews) is notable.

As to the blurring and camouflaging of the self, it is achieved solely by imitation—by becoming as like others as possible. The desire to belong is partly a desire to lose oneself.

Finally, the lack of self-confidence characteristic of the frustrated also stimulates their imitativeness. The more we mistrust our judgment and luck, the more are we ready to follow the example of others.

79

Mere rejection of the self, even when not accompanied by a search for a new identity, can lead to increased imitativeness. The rejected self ceases to assert its claim to distinctness, and there is nothing to resist the propensity to copy. The situation is not unlike that observed in children and undifferentiated adults where the lack of a distinct individuality leaves the mind without guards against the intrusion of influences from without.

80

A feeling of superiority counteracts imitation. Had the millions of immigrants who came to this country been superior people—the cream of the countries they came from—there would have been not one U.S.A. but a mosaic of lingual and cultural groups. It was due to the fact that the majority of the immigrants were of the lowest and the poorest, the despised and the rejected, that the heterogeneous millions blended so rapidly and thoroughly. They came here with the ardent desire to shed their old world identity and be reborn to a new life; and they were automatically equipped with an unbounded capacity to imitate and adopt the new. The strangeness of the new country attracted rather than repelled them. They craved a new identity and a new life—and the stranger the new world the more it suited their inclination. Perhaps, to the non-Anglo-Saxons, the strangeness of the language was an added attraction. To have to learn to speak enhanced the illusion of being born anew.

81

Imitation is often a shortcut to a solution. We copy when we lack the inclination, the ability or the time to work out an independent solution. People in a hurry will imitate more readily than people at leisure. Hustling thus tends to produce uniformity. And in the deliberate fusing of individuals into a compact group, incessant action will play a considerable role.[22]

82

Unification of itself, whether brought about by persuasion, coercion or spontaneous surrender, tends to intensify the imitation capacity. A civilian drafted into the army and made a member of a close-knit military unit becomes more imitative than he was in civilian life. The unified individual is without a distinct self; he is perennially incomplete and immature, and therefore without resistance against influences from without. The marked imitativeness of primitive people is perhaps due less to their primitiveness than to the fact that they are usually members of compact clans or tribes.

The ready imitativeness of a unified following is both an advantage and a peril to a mass movement. The faithful are easily led and molded, but they are also particularly susceptible to foreign influences. One has the impression that a thoroughly unified group is easily seduced and corrupted. The preaching of all mass movements bristles with admonitions against copying foreign models and "doing after all their abominations." The imitation of outsiders is branded as treason and apostasy. "Whoever copies a foreigner is guilty of *lèse-nation* (an insult to the nation) like a spy who admits an enemy by a secret doorway."[23] Every device is used to cut off the faithful from intercourse with unbelievers. Some mass movements go to the extreme of leading their following into the wilderness in order to allow an undisturbed settling of the new pattern of life.

Contempt for the outside world is of course the most effective defense against disruptive imitation. However, an active mass movement prizes hatred above passive contempt; and hatred does not stifle imitation but often stimulates it (see Section 73). Only in the case of small corporate bodies enclosed in a sea of foreignness, and intent solely on preserving their distinctness, is contempt employed as an insulator. It leads to an exclusiveness inhospitable to converts.

The imitativeness of its members gives a thoroughly unified group great flexibility and adaptability. It can adopt innovations and change its orientation with astounding ease. The rapid modernization of a united Japan or Turkey contrasts markedly with the slow and painful adaptation to new ways in China, Iran and other countries not animated by a spirit of unity. A thoroughly unified Soviet Russia has a better chance of assimilating new methods and a new way of life than the loosely joined Russia of the Czars. It is also obvious that a primitive people with an intact collective framework can be more readily modernized than one with a crumbling tribal or communal pattern.[24]

PERSUASION AND COERCION

83

We tend today to exaggerate the effectiveness of persuasion as a means of inculcating opinion and shaping behavior. We see in propaganda a formidable instrument. To its skillful use we attribute many of the startling successes of the mass movements of our time, and we have come to fear the word as much as the sword.

Actually the fabulous effects ascribed to propaganda have no greater foundation in fact than the fall of the walls of Jericho ascribed to the blast of Joshua's trumpets. Were propaganda by itself one-tenth as potent as it is made out to be, the totalitarian regimes of Russia, Germany, Italy and Spain would have been mild affairs. They would have been blatant and brazen but without the ghastly brutality of secret police, concentration camps and mass extermination.

The truth seems to be that propaganda on its own cannot force its way into unwilling minds; neither can it inculcate something wholly new; nor can it keep people persuaded once they have ceased to believe. It penetrates only into minds already open, and rather than instill opinion it articulates and justifies opinions already present in the minds of its recipients. The gifted propagandist brings to a boil ideas and passions already simmering in the minds of his hearers. He echoes their innermost feelings. Where opinion is not coerced, people can be made to believe only in what they already "know."

Propaganda by itself succeeds mainly with the frustrated. Their throbbing fears, hopes and passions crowd at the portals of their senses and get between them and the outside world. They cannot see but what they have already imagined, and it is the music of their own souls they hear in the impassioned words of the propagandist. Indeed, it is easier for the frustrated to detect their own imaginings and hear the echo of their own musings in impassioned double-talk and sonorous refrains than in precise words joined together with faultless logic.

Propaganda by itself, however skillful, cannot keep people persuaded once they have ceased to believe. To maintain itself, a mass movement has to order things so that when the people no longer believe, they can be made to believe by force.[25]

As we shall see later (Section 104), words are an essential instrument in preparing the ground for a mass movement. But once the movement is realized, words, though still useful, cease to play a decisive role. So acknowledged a master of propaganda as Dr. Goebbels admits in an unguarded moment that "A sharp sword must always stand behind propaganda if it is to be really effective."[26] He also sounds apologetic when he claims that "it cannot be denied that more can be done with good propaganda than by no propaganda at all."[27]

84

Contrary to what one would expect, propaganda becomes more fervent and importunate when it operates in conjunction with coercion than when it has to rely solely on its own effectiveness.

Both they who convert and they who are converted by coercion need the fervent conviction that the faith they impose or are forced to adopt is the only true one. Without this conviction, the proselytizing terrorist, if he is not vicious to begin with, is likely to feel a criminal, and the coerced convert see himself as a coward who prostituted his soul to live.

Propaganda thus serves more to justify ourselves than to convince others; and the more reason we have to feel guilty, the more fervent our propaganda.

85

It is probably as true that violence breeds fanaticism as that fanaticism begets violence. It is often impossible to tell which came first. Both those who employ violence and those subject to it are likely to develop a fanatical state of mind. Ferrero says of the terrorists of the French Revolution that the more blood they "shed the more they needed to believe in their principles as absolutes. Only the absolute might still absolve them in their own eyes and sustain their desperate energy. [They] did not spill all that blood because they believed in popular sovereignty as a religious truth; they tried to believe in popular sovereignty as a religious truth because their fear made them spill so much blood."[28] The practice of terror serves the true believer not only to cow and crush his opponents but also to invigorate and intensify his own faith. Every lynching in our South not only intimidates the Negro but also invigorates the fanatical conviction of white supremacy.

In the case of the coerced, too, violence can beget fanaticism. There is evidence that the coerced convert is often as fanatical in his adherence to the new faith as the persuaded convert, and sometimes even more so. It is not always true that "He who complies against his will is of his own opinion still." Islam imposed its faith by force, yet the coerced Muslims displayed a devotion to the new faith more ardent than that of the first Arabs engaged in the movement. According to Renan, Islam obtained from its coerced converts "a faith ever tending to grow stronger."[29] Fanatical orthodoxy is in all movements a late development. It comes when the movement is in full possession of power and can impose its faith by force as well as by persuasion.

Thus coercion when implacable and persistent has an unequaled persuasiveness, and this not only with simple souls but also with those who pride themselves on the strength and integrity of their intellect. When an arbitrary decree from the Kremlin forces scientists, writers, and artists to recant their convictions and confess their errors, the chances are that such recantations and confessions represent genuine conversions rather than lip service. It needs fanatical faith to rationalize our cowardice.

86

There is hardly an example of a mass movement achieving vast proportions and a durable organization solely by persuasion. Professor K. S. Latourette, a very Christian historian, has to admit that "However incompatible the spirit of Jesus and armed force may be, and however unpleasant it may be to acknowledge the fact, as a matter of plain history the latter has often made it possible for the former to survive."[30] It was the temporal sword that made Christianity a world religion. Conquest and conversion went hand in hand, the latter often serving as a justification and a tool for the former. Where Christianity failed to gain or retain the backing of state power, it achieved neither a wide nor a permanent hold. "In Persia . . . Christianity confronted a state religion sustained by the crown and never became the faith of more than a minority."[31] In the phenomenal spread of Islam, conquest was a primary factor and conversion a by-product. "The most flourishing periods for Mohammedanism have been at the times of its greatest political ascendancy; and it is at those times that it has received its largest accession from without."[32] The Reformation made headway only where it gained the backing of the ruling prince or the local government. Said Melanchthon, Luther's wisest lieutenant: "Without the intervention of the civil authority what would our precepts become?—Platonic laws."[33] Where, as in France, the state power was against it, it was drowned in blood and never rose again. In the case of the French Revolution, "It was the armies of the Revolution, not its ideas, that penetrated throughout the whole of Europe."[34] There was no question of intellectual contagion. Dumouriez protested that the French proclaimed the sacred law of liberty "like the Koran, sword in hand."[35] The threat of communism at present does not come from the forcefulness of its preaching but from the fact that it is backed by one of the mightiest armies on earth.

It also seems that, where a mass movement can either persuade or coerce, it usually chooses the latter. Persuasion is clumsy and its results uncertain. Said the Spaniard St. Dominic to the heretical Albigenses: "For many years I have exhorted you in vain, with gentleness, preaching, praying and weeping. But according to the proverb of my country, 'where blessing can accomplish nothing, blows may avail.' We shall rouse against you princes and prelates, who, alas, will arm nations and kingdoms against this land ... and thus blows will avail where blessings and gentleness have been powerless."[36]

87

The assertion that a mass movement cannot be stopped by force is not literally true. Force can stop and crush even the most vigorous movement. But to do so the force must be ruthless and persistent. And here is where faith enters as an indispensable factor. For a persecution that is ruthless and persistent can come only from fanatical conviction. "Any violence which does not spring from a firm, spiritual base, will be wavering and uncertain. It lacks the stability which can only rest in a fanatical outlook."[37] The terrorism which emanates from individual brutality neither goes far enough nor lasts long enough. It is spasmodic, subject to moods and hesitations. "But as soon as force wavers and alternates with forbearance, not only will the doctrine to be repressed recover again and again, but it will also be in a position to draw new benefit from every persecution."[38] The holy terror only knows no limit and never flags.

Thus it seems that we need ardent faith not only to be able to resist coercion,[39] but also to be able to exercise it effectively.

88

Whence comes the impulse to proselytize?

Intensity of conviction is not the main factor which impels a movement to spread its faith to the four corners of the earth: "religions of great intensity often confine themselves to contemning, destroying, or at best pitying what is not themselves."[40] Nor is the impulse to proselytize an expression of an overabundance of power which as Bacon has it "is like a great flood, that will be sure to overflow."[41] The missionary zeal seems rather an expression of some deep misgiving, some pressing feeling of insufficiency at the center. Proselytizing is more a passionate search for something not yet found than a desire to bestow upon the world something we already have. It is a search for a final and irrefutable demonstration that our absolute truth is indeed the one and only truth. The proselytizing fanatic strengthens his own faith by converting others. The creed whose legitimacy is most easily challenged is likely to develop the strongest proselytizing impulse. It is doubtful whether a movement which does not profess some preposterous and patently irrational dogma can be possessed of that zealous drive which "must either win men or destroy the world." It is also plausible that those movements with the greatest inner contradiction between profession and practice—that is to say with a strong feeling of guilt— are likely to be the most fervent in imposing their faith on others. The more unworkable communism proves in Russia, and the more its leaders are compelled to compromise and adulterate the original creed, the more brazen and arrogant will be their attack on a non-believing world. The slaveholders of the South became the more aggressive in spreading their way of life the more it became patent that their position was untenable in a modern world. If free enterprise becomes a proselytizing holy cause, it will be a sign that its workability and advantages have ceased to be self-evident.

The passion for proselytizing and the passion for world dominion are both perhaps symptoms of some serious deficiency at the center. It is probably as true of a band of apostles or conquistadors as it is of a band of fugitives setting out for a distant land that they escape from an untenable situation at home. And how often indeed do the three meet, mingle and exchange their parts.

LEADERSHIP

89

No matter how vital we think the role of leadership in the rise of a mass movement, there is no doubt that the leader cannot create the conditions which make the rise of a movement possible. He cannot conjure a movement out of the void. There has to be an eagerness to follow and obey, and an intense dissatisfaction with things as they are, before movement and leader can make their appearance. When conditions are not ripe, the potential leader, no matter how gifted, and his holy cause, no matter how potent, remain without a following. The First World War and its aftermath readied the ground for the rise of the Bolshevik, Fascist and Nazi movements. Had the war been averted or postponed a decade or two, the fate of Lenin, Mussolini and Hitler would not have been different from that of the brilliant plotters and agitators of the nineteenth century who never succeeded in ripening the frequent disorders and crises of their time into full-scale mass movements. Something was lacking. The European masses up to the cataclysmic events of the First World War had not utterly despaired of the present and were, therefore, not willing to sacrifice it for a new life and a new world. Even the nationalist leaders, who fared better than the revolutionists, did not succeed in making of nationalism the popular holy cause it has become since. Militant nationalism and militant revolutionism seem to be contemporaneous.

In Britain, too, the leader had to wait for the times to ripen before he could play his role. During the 1930's the potential leader (Churchill) was prominent in the eyes of the people and made himself heard, day in, day out. But the will to follow was not there. It was only when disaster shook the country to its foundation and made autonomous individual lives untenable and meaningless that the leader came into his own.

There is a period of waiting in the wings—often a very long period—for all the great leaders whose entrance on the scene seems to us a most crucial point in the course of a mass movement. Accidents and the activities of other men have to set the stage for them before they can enter and start their performance. "The commanding man in a momentous day seems only to be the last accident in a series."[42]

90

Once the stage is set, the presence of an outstanding leader is indispensable. Without him there will be no movement. The ripeness of the times does not automatically produce a mass movement, nor can elections, laws and administrative bureaus hatch one. It was Lenin who forced the flow of events into the channels of the Bolshevik revolution. Had he died in Switzerland, or on his way to Russia in 1917, it is almost certain that the other prominent Bolsheviks would have joined a coalition government. The result might have been a more or less liberal republic run chiefly by the bourgeoisie. In the case of Mussolini and Hitler the evidence is even more decisive: without them there would have been neither a Fascist nor a Nazi movement.

Events in England at this moment also demonstrate the indispensability of a gifted leader for the crystallization of a mass movement. A genuine leader (a Socialist Churchill) at the head of the Labor government would have initiated the drastic reforms of nationalization in the fervent atmosphere of a mass movement and not in the undramatic drabness of Socialist austerity. He would have cast the British worker in the role of a heroic producer and in that of a pioneer in truly scientific industrialism. He would have made the British feel that their chief task is to show the whole world, and America and Russia in particular, what a truly civilized nation can do with modern methods of production when free alike from the confusion, waste and greed of capitalist management and from the byzantinism, barbarism and ignorance of a Bolshevik bureaucracy. He would have known how to infuse the British people with the same pride and hope which sustained them in the darkest hours of the war.

It needs the iron will, daring and vision of an exceptional leader to concert and mobilize existing attitudes and impulses into the collective drive of a mass movement. The leader personifies the certitude of the creed and the defiance and grandeur of power. He articulates and justifies the resentment dammed up in the souls of the frustrated. He kindles the vision of a breathtaking future so as to justify the sacrifice of a transitory present. He stages the world of make-believe so indispensable for the realization of self-sacrifice and united action. He evokes the enthusiasm of communion—the sense of liberation from a petty and meaningless individual existence.

What are the talents requisite for such a performance? Exceptional intelligence, noble character and originality seem neither indispensable nor perhaps desirable. The main requirements seem to be: audacity and a joy in defiance; an iron will; a fanatical conviction that he is in possession of the one and only truth; faith in his destiny and luck; a capacity for passionate hatred; contempt for the present; a cunning estimate of human nature; a delight in symbols (spectacles and ceremonials); unbounded brazenness which finds expression in a disregard of consistency and fairness; a recognition that the innermost craving of a following is for communion and that there can never be too much of it; a capacity for winning and holding the utmost loyalty of a group of able lieutenants. This last faculty is one of the most essential and elusive. The uncanny powers of a leader manifest themselves not so much in the hold he has on the masses as in his ability to dominate and almost bewitch a small group of able men. These men must be fearless, proud, intelligent and capable of organizing and running large-scale undertakings, and yet they must submit wholly to the will of the leader, draw their inspiration and driving force from him, and glory in this submission.

Not all the qualities enumerated above are equally essential. The most decisive for the effectiveness of a mass movement leader seem to be audacity, fanatical faith in a holy cause, an awareness of the importance of a close-knit collectivity, and, above all, the ability to evoke fervent devotion in a group of able lieutenants. Trotsky's failure as a leader came from his neglect, or more probably his inability, to create a machine of able and loyal lieutenants. He did not attract personal sympathies, or if he did he could not keep them.[43] An additional shortcoming was his ineradicable respect for the individual, particularly the creative individual. He was not convinced of the sinfulness and ineffectuality of an autonomous individual existence and did not grasp the overwhelming importance of communion to a mass movement. Sun Yat-sen "attracted to himself . . . an extraordinary number of able and devoted followers, firing their imaginations with his visions of the new China and compelling loyalty and self-sacrifice."[44] Unlike him, Chiang Kai-shek seems to lack every essential quality of a mass movement leader. On the other hand, de Gaulle is certainly a man to watch. The leaders of Communist parties outside Russia, by their subservience to Stalin and the Politburo cannot attain the status of genuine leaders. They remain able lieutenants. For communism to become at present an effective mass movement in any Western country, one of two opposites has to happen. Either the personality of Stalin is made so tangible and immediate that it can act as a catalyst, or the local Communist party has to cut loose from Russia and, after the manner of Tito, flaunt its defiance against both capitalism and Stalinism. Had Lenin been the emissary of a leader and a politburo sitting in some distant foreign land, it is doubtful whether he could have exercised his fateful influence on the course of events in Russia.

91

The crude ideas advanced by many of the successful mass movement leaders of our time incline one to assume that a certain coarseness and immaturity of mind is an asset to leadership. However, it was not the intellectual crudity of an Aimee McPherson or a Hitler which won and held their following but the boundless self-confidence which prompted these leaders to give full rein to their preposterous ideas. A genuinely wise leader who dared to follow out the course of his wisdom would have an equal chance of success. The quality of ideas seems to play a minor role in mass movement leadership. What counts is the arrogant gesture, the complete disregard of the opinion of others, the singlehanded defiance of the world.

Charlatanism of some degree is indispensable to effective leadership. There can be no mass movement without some deliberate misrepresentation of facts. No solid, tangible advantage can hold a following and make it zealous and loyal unto death. The leader has to be practical and a realist, yet must talk the language of the visionary and the idealist.

Originality is not a prerequisite of great mass movement leadership. One of the most striking traits of the successful mass movement leader is his readiness to imitate both friend and foe, both past and contemporary models. The daring which is essential to this type of leadership consists as much in the daring to imitate as in the daring to defy the world. Perhaps the clue to any heroic career is an unbounded capacity for imitation; a single-minded fashioning after a model. This excessive capacity for imitation indicates that the hero is without a fully developed and realized self. There is much in him that is rudimentary and suppressed. His strength lies in his blind spots and in plugging all outlets but one.

92

The total surrender of a distinct self is a prerequisite for the attainment of both unity and self-sacrifice; and there is probably no more direct way of realizing this surrender than by inculcating and extolling the habit of blind obedience. When Stalin forces scientists, writers and artists to crawl on their bellies and deny their individual intelligence, sense of beauty and moral sense, he is not indulging a sadistic impulse but is solemnizing, in a most impressive way, the supreme virtue of blind obedience. All mass movements rank obedience with the highest virtues and put it on a level with faith: "union of minds requires not only a perfect accord in the one Faith, but complete submission and obedience of will to the Church and the Roman Pontiff as to God Himself."[45] Obedience is not only the first law of God, but also the first tenet of a revolutionary party and of fervent nationalism. "Not to reason why" is considered by all mass movements the mark of a strong and generous spirit.

The disorder, bloodshed and destruction which mark the trail of a rising mass movement lead us to think of the followers of the movement as being by nature rowdy and lawless. Actually, mass ferocity is not always the sum of individual lawlessness. Personal truculence militates against united action. It moves the individual to strike out for himself. It produces the pioneer, adventurer and bandit. The true believer, no matter how rowdy and violent his acts, is basically an obedient and submissive person.

The Christian converts who staged razzias against the University of Alexandria and lynched professors suspected of unorthodoxy were submissive members of a compact church. The Communist rioter is a servile member of a party. Both the Japanese and Nazi rowdies were the most disciplined people the world has seen. In this country, the American employer often finds in the racial fanatic of our South—so given to mass violence—a respectful and docile factory hand. The army, too, finds him particularly amenable to discipline.

93

People whose lives are barren and insecure seem to show a greater willingness to obey than people who are self-sufficient and self-confident. To the frustrated, freedom from responsibility is more attractive than freedom from restraint. They are eager to barter their independence for relief from the burdens of willing, deciding and being responsible for inevitable failure. They willingly abdicate the directing of their lives to those who want to plan, command and shoulder all responsibility. Moreover, submission by all to a supreme leader is an approach to their ideal of equality.

In time of crisis, during floods, earthquakes, epidemics, depressions and wars, separate individual effort is of no avail, and people of every condition are ready to obey and follow a leader. To obey is then the only firm point in a chaotic day-by-day existence.

94

The frustrated are also likely to be the most steadfast followers. It is remarkable, that, in a co-operative effort, the least self-reliant are the least likely to be discouraged by defeat. For they join others in a common undertaking not so much to ensure the success of a cherished project as to avoid an individual shouldering of blame in case of failure. When the common undertaking fails, they are still spared the one thing they fear most, namely, the showing up of their individual shortcomings. Their faith remains unimpaired and they are eager to follow in a new attempt.

The frustrated follow a leader less because of their faith that he is leading them to a promised land than because of their immediate feeling that he is leading them away from their unwanted selves. Surrender to a leader is not a means to an end but a fulfillment. Whither they are led is of secondary importance.

95

There is probably a crucial difference between a mass movement leader and a leader in a free society. In a more or less free society, the leader can retain his hold on the people only when he has blind faith in their wisdom and goodness. A second-rate leader possessed of this faith will outlast a first-rate leader who is without it. This means that in a free society the leader follows the people even as he leads them. He must, as someone said, find out where the people are going so that he may lead them. When the leader in a free society becomes contemptuous of the people, he sooner or later proceeds on the false and fatal theory that all men are fools, and eventually blunders into defeat. Things are different where the leader can employ ruthless coercion. Where, as in an active mass movement, the leader can exact blind obedience, he can operate on the sound theory that all men are cowards, treat them accordingly and get results.

One of the reasons that Communist leaders are losing out in our unions is that by following the line and adopting the tactics of the party, they are assuming the attitude and using the tactics of a mass movement leader in an organization made up of free men.

ACTION

96

Action is a unifier. There is less individual distinctness in the genuine man of action—the builder, soldier, sportsman and even the scientist—than in the thinker or in one whose creativeness flows from communion with the self. The go-getter and the hustler have much in them that is abortive and undifferentiated. One is never really stripped for action unless one is stripped of a distinct and differentiated self. An active people thus tends toward uniformity. It is doubtful whether without the vast action involved in the conquest of a continent, our nation of immigrants could have attained its amazing homogeneity in so short a time. Those who came to this country to act (to make money) were more quickly and thoroughly Americanized than those who came to realize some lofty ideal. The former felt an immediate kinship with the millions absorbed in the same pursuit. It was as if they were joining a brotherhood. They recognized early that in order to succeed they had to blend with their fellow men, do as others do, learn the lingo and play the game. Moreover, the mad rush in which they joined prevented the unfolding of their being, so that, without a distinct individuality, they could not, even if they had been so inclined, put up an effective resistance against the influence of their new environment.[46] On the other hand, those who came to this country to realize an ideal (of freedom, justice, equality) measured the realities of the new land against their ideal and found them wanting. They felt superior, and inevitably insulated themselves against the new environment.

97

Men of thought seldom work well together, whereas between men of action there is usually an easy camaraderie. Teamwork is rare in intellectual or artistic undertakings, but common and almost indispensable among men of action. The cry "Go to, let us build us a city, and a tower"[47] is always a call for united action. A Communist commissar of industry has probably more in common with a capitalist industrialist than with a Communist theoretician. The real International is that of men of action.

98

All mass movements avail themselves of action as a means of unification. The conflicts a mass movement seeks and incites serve not only to down its enemies but also to strip its followers of their distinct individuality and render them more soluble in the collective medium. Clearing of land, building of cities, exploration and large-scale industrial undertakings serve a similar purpose. Even mere marching can serve as a unifier. The Nazis made vast use of this preposterous variant of action. Hermann Rauschning, who at first thought this eternal marching a senseless waste of time and energy, recognized later its subtle effect. "Marching diverts men's thoughts. Marching kills thought. Marching makes an end of individuality."[48]

A mass movement's call for action evokes an eager

response in the frustrated. For the frustrated see in action a cure for all that ails them. It brings self-forgetting and it gives them a sense of purpose and worth. Indeed it seems that frustration stems chiefly from an inability to act, and that the most poignantly frustrated are those whose talents and temperament equip them ideally for a life of action but are condemned by circumstances to rust away in idleness. How else explain the surprising fact that the Lenins, Trotskys, Mussolinis and Hitlers who spent the best part of their lives talking their heads off in cafés and meetings reveal themselves suddenly as the most able and tireless men of action of their time?

99

Faith organizes and equips man's soul for action. To be in possession of the one and only truth and never doubt one's righteousness; to feel that one is backed by a mysterious power whether it be God, destiny or the law of history; to be convinced that one's opponents are the incarnation of evil and must be crushed; to exult in self-denial and devotion to duty—these are admirable qualifications for resolute and ruthless action in any field. Psalm-singing soldiers, pioneers, businessmen and even sportsmen have proved themselves formidable. Revolutionary and nationalist enthusiasms have a similar effect: they, too, can turn spiritless and inert people into fighters and builders. Here then is another reason for the apparent indispensability of a mass movement in the modernization of backward and stagnant countries.

However, the exceptional fitness of the true believer for a life of action can be as much a danger as an aid to the prospects of a mass movement. By opening vast fields of feverish action a mass movement may hasten its end.

Successful action tends to become an end in itself. It drains all energies and fervors into its own channels. Faith and holy cause, instead of being the supreme purpose, become mere lubricants for the machine of action. The true believer who succeeds in all he does gains self-confidence and becomes reconciled with his self and the present. He no longer sees his only salvation in losing himself in the oneness of a corporate body and in becoming an anonymous particle with no will, judgment and responsibility of his own. He seeks and finds his salvation in action, in proving his worth and in asserting his individual superiority. Action cannot lead him to self-realization, but he readily finds in it self-justification. If he still hangs on to his faith, it is but to bolster his confidence and legitimatize his success. Thus the taste of continuous successful action is fatal to the spirit of collectivity. A people steeped in action is likely to be the least religious, the least revolutionary and the least chauvinist. The social stability and the political and religious tolerance of the Anglo-Saxon peoples is due in part to the relative abundance among them of the will, skill and opportunities for action. Action served them as a substitute for a mass movement.

There is of course the constant danger that should the avenues of action be thoroughly blocked by a severe depression or defeat in war the resulting frustration is likely to be so intense that almost any proselytizing mass movement would find the situation ready-made for its propagation. The explosive situation in Germany after the First World War was partly due to the inactivity forced upon a population that knew itself admirably equipped for action. Hitler gave them a mass movement. But what was probably more important, he opened before them unlimited opportunities for feverish, incessant and spectacular action. No wonder they heiled him as their Savior.

SUSPICION

100

We have seen that the acrid secretion of the frustrated mind, though composed chiefly of fear and ill will, acts yet as a marvelous slime to cement the embittered and disaffected into one compact whole. Suspicion too is an ingredient of this acrid slime, and it too can act as a unifying agent.

The awareness of their individual blemishes and shortcomings inclines the frustrated to detect ill will and meanness in their fellow men. Self-contempt, however vague, sharpens our eyes for the imperfections of others. We usually strive to reveal in others the blemishes we hide in ourselves. Thus when the frustrated congregate in a mass movement, the air is heavy-laden with suspicion. There is prying and spying, tense watching and a tense awareness of being watched. The surprising thing is that this pathological mistrust within the ranks leads not to dissension but to strict conformity. Knowing themselves continually watched, the faithful strive to escape suspicion by adhering zealously to prescribed behavior and opinion. Strict orthodoxy is as much the result of mutual suspicion as of ardent faith.

Mass movements make extensive use of suspicion in their machinery of domination. The rank-and-file within the Nazi party were made to feel that they were continually under observation and were kept in a permanent state of uneasy conscience and fear.[49] Fear of one's neighbors, one's friends and even one's relatives seems to be the rule within all mass movements. Now and then innocent people are deliberately accused and sacrificed in order to keep suspicion alive. Suspicion is given a sharp edge by associating all opposition within the ranks with the enemy threatening the movement from without. This enemy—the indispensable devil of every mass movement—is omnipresent. He plots both outside and inside the ranks of the faithful. It is his voice that speaks through the mouth of the dissenter, and the deviationists are his stooges. If anything goes wrong within the movement, it is his doing. It is the sacred duty of the true believer to be suspicious. He must be constantly on the lookout for saboteurs, spies and traitors.

101

Collective unity is not the result of the brotherly love of the faithful for each other. The loyalty of the true believer is to the whole—the church, party, nation—and not to his fellow true believer. True loyalty between individuals is possible only in a loose and relatively free society. As Abraham was ready to sacrifice his only son to prove his devotion to Jehovah, so must the fanatical Nazi or Communist be ready to sacrifice relatives and friends to demonstrate his total surrender to the holy cause. The active mass movement sees in the personal ties of blood and friendship a diminution of its own corporate cohesion. Thus mutual suspicion within the ranks is not only compatible with corporate strength, but, one might almost say, a precondition of it. "Men of strong convictions and strong passions, when leagued together, watch one another with suspicion, and find their strength in it; for mutual suspicion creates mutual dread, binds them as by an iron band, prevents desertion, and braces them against moments of weakness."[50]

It is part of the formidableness of a genuine mass movement that the self-sacrifice it promotes includes also a sacrifice of some of the moral sense which cramps and restrains our nature. "Our zeal works wonders when it

seconds our propensity to hatred, cruelty, ambition, ava-
rice, detraction, rebellion."[51]

THE EFFECTS OF UNIFICATION

102

Thorough unification, whether brought about by spontaneous surrender, persuasion, coercion, necessity or in-
grained habit, or a combination of these, tends to intensify
the inclinations and attitudes which promote unity. We
have seen that unification intensifies the propensity to
hatred (Section 77) and the imitative capacity (Section 82).
It is also true that the unified individual is more credulous
and obedient than the potential true believer who is still
an autonomous individual. Though it is true that the leadership of a collective body usually keeps hatred at a white
heat, encourages imitation and credulity and fosters obedience, the fact remains that unification by itself, even
when not aided by the manipulations of the leadership,
intensifies the reactions which function as unifying
agents.

This at first sight is a surprising fact. We have seen that
most unifying factors originate in the revulsion of the frustrated individual from an unwanted self and an untenable
existence. But the true believer who is wholly assimilated
into a compact collective body is no longer frustrated. He
has found a new identity and a new life. He is one of the
chosen, bolstered and protected by invincible powers,
and destined to inherit the earth. His is a state of mind the
very opposite of that of the frustrated individual; yet he
displays, with increased intensity, all the reactions which
are symptomatic of inner tension and insecurity.

What happens to the unified individual?

Unification is more a process of diminution than of addition. In order to be assimilated into a collective medium a person has to be stripped of his individual distinctness. He has to be deprived of free choice and independent judgment. Many of his natural bents and impulses have to be suppressed or blunted. All these are acts of diminution. The elements which are apparently added—faith, hope, pride, confidence—are negative in origin. The exaltation of the true believer does not flow from reserves of strength and wisdom but from a sense of deliverance: he has been delivered from the meaningless burdens of an autonomous existence. "We Germans are so happy. We are free from freedom."[52] His happiness and fortitude come from his no longer being himself. Attacks against the self cannot touch him. His powers of endurance when at the mercy of an implacable enemy or when facing insupportable circumstances are superior to those of an autonomous individual. But this invincibility depends upon the life line which connects him with the collective whole. As long as he feels himself part of that whole and nothing else, he is indestructible and immortal. All his fervor and fanaticism are, therefore, clustered around this life line. His striving for utmost unity is more intense than the vague longing of the frustrated for an escape from an untenable self. The frustrated individual still has a choice: he can find a new life not only by becoming part of a corporate body but also by changing his environment or by throwing himself wholeheartedly into some absorbing undertaking. The unified individual, on the other hand, has no choice. He must cling to the collective body or like a fallen leaf wither and fade. It is doubtful whether the excommunicated priest, the expelled Communist and the renegade chauvinist can ever find peace of mind as autonomous individuals. They cannot stand on their own, but must embrace a new cause and attach themselves to a new group.

The true believer is eternally incomplete, eternally insecure.

103

It is of interest to note the means by which a mass movement accentuates and perpetuates the individual incompleteness of its adherents. By elevating dogma above reason, the individual's intelligence is prevented from becoming self-reliant. Economic dependence is maintained by centralizing economic power and by a deliberately created scarcity of the necessities of life. Social self-sufficiency is discouraged by crowded housing or communal quarters, and by enforced daily participation in public functions. Ruthless censorship of literature, art, music and science prevents even the creative few from living self-sufficient lives. The inculcated devotions to church, party, country, leader and creed also perpetuate a state of incompleteness. For every devotion is a socket which demands the fitting in of a complementary part from without.

Thus people raised in the atmosphere of a mass movement are fashioned into incomplete and dependent human beings even when they have within themselves the making of self-sufficient entities. Though strangers to frustration and without a grievance, they will yet exhibit the peculiarities of people who crave to lose themselves and be rid of an existence that is irrevocably spoiled.

PART 4

Beginning and End

XV

Men of Words

104

Mass movements do not usually rise until the prevailing order has been discredited. The discrediting is not an automatic result of the blunders and abuses of those in power, but the deliberate work of men of words with a grievance. Where the articulate are absent or without a grievance, the prevailing dispensation, though incompetent and corrupt, may continue in power until it falls and crumbles of itself. On the other hand, a dispensation of undoubted merit and vigor may be swept away if it fails to win the allegiance of the articulate minority.[1]

As pointed out in Sections 83 and 86, the realization and perpetuation of a mass movement depend on force. A full-blown mass movement is a ruthless affair, and its management is in the hands of ruthless fanatics who use words only to give an appearance of spontaneity to a consent obtained by coercion. But these fanatics can move in and take charge only after the prevailing order has been discredited and has lost the allegiance of the masses. The preliminary work of undermining existing institutions, of familiarizing the masses with the idea of change, and of creating a receptivity to a new faith, can be done only by men who are, first and foremost, talkers or writers and are recognized as such by all. As long as the existing order functions in a more or less orderly fashion, the masses remain basically conservative. They can think of reform but not of total innovation. The fanatical extremist, no matter how eloquent, strikes them as dangerous, traitorous, impractical or even insane. They will not listen to him. Lenin himself recognized that where the ground is not ready for them the Communists "find it hard to approach the masses . . . and even get them to listen to them."[2] Moreover, the authorities, even when feeble or tolerant, are likely to react violently against the activist tactics of the fanatic and may gain from his activities, as it were, a new vigor.

Things are different in the case of the typical man of words. The masses listen to him because they know that his words, however urgent, cannot have immediate results. The authorities either ignore him or use mild methods to muzzle him. Thus imperceptibly the man of words undermines established institutions, discredits those in power, weakens prevailing beliefs and loyalties, and sets the stage for the rise of a mass movement.

The division between men of words, fanatics and practical men of action, as outlined in the following sections, is not meant to be categorical. Men like Gandhi and Trotsky start out as apparently ineffectual men of words and later display exceptional talents as administrators or generals. A man like Mohammed starts out as a man of words, develops into an implacable fanatic and finally reveals a superb practical sense. A fanatic like Lenin is a master of the spoken word and unequaled as a man of action. What the classification attempts to suggest is that the readying of the ground for a mass movement is done best by men whose chief claim to excellence is their skill in the use of the spoken or written word; that the hatching of an actual movement requires the temperament and the talents of the fanatic; and that the final consolidation of the movement is largely the work of practical men of action.

The emergence of an articulate minority where there was none before is a potential revolutionary step. The Western powers were indirect and unknowing fomenters of mass movements in Asia not only by kindling resentment (see Section 1) but also by creating articulate minorities through educational work which was largely philanthropic. Many of the revolutionary leaders in India, China and Indonesia received their training in conservative Western institutions. The American college at Beirut, which is directed and supported by Godfearing, conservative Americans, is a school for revolutionaries in the illiterate Arabic world. Nor is there any doubt that the Godfearing missionary school teachers in China were unknowingly among those who prepared the ground for the Chinese revolution.

105

The men of words are of diverse types. They can be priests, scribes, prophets, writers, artists, professors, students and intellectuals in general. Where, as in China, reading and writing is a difficult art, mere literacy can give one the status of a man of words. A similar situation prevailed in ancient Egypt, where the art of picture writing was the monopoly of a minority.

Whatever the type, there is a deep-seated craving common to almost all men of words which determines their attitude to the prevailing order. It is a craving for recognition; a craving for a clearly marked status above the common run of humanity. "Vanity," said Napoleon, "made the Revolution; liberty was only a pretext." There is apparently an irremediable insecurity at the core of every intellectual, be he noncreative or creative. Even the most gifted and prolific seem to live a life of eternal self-doubting and have to prove their worth anew each day. What de Rémusat said of Thiers is perhaps true of most men of words: "he has much more vanity than ambition; and he prefers consideration to obedience, and the appearance of power to power itself. Consult him constantly, and then do just as you please. He will take more notice of your deference to him than of your actions."[3]

There is a moment in the career of almost every faultfinding man of words when a deferential or conciliatory gesture from those in power may win him over to their side. At a certain stage, most men of words are ready to become timeservers and courtiers. Jesus Himself might not have preached a new Gospel had the dominant Pharisees taken Him into the fold, called Him Rabbi, and listened to Him with deference. A bishopric conferred on Luther at the right moment might have cooled his ardor for a Reformation. The young Karl Marx could perhaps have been won over to Prussiandom by the bestowal of a title and an important government job; and Lassalle, by a title and a court uniform. It is true that once the man of words formulates a philosophy and a program, he is likely to stand by them and be immune to blandishments and enticements.

However much the protesting man of words sees himself as the champion of the downtrodden and injured, the grievance which animates him is, with very few exceptions, private and personal. His pity is usually hatched out of his hatred for the powers that be.[4] "It is only a few rare and exceptional men who have that kind of love toward mankind at large that makes them unable to endure patiently the general mass of evil and suffering, regardless of any relation it may have to their own lives."[5] Thoreau states the fact with fierce extravagance: "I believe that

what so saddens the reformer is not his sympathy with his
fellows in distress, but, though he be the holiest son of
God, is his private ail. Let this be righted . . . and he will
forsake his generous companions without apology."[6]
When his superior status is suitably acknowledged by
those in power, the man of words usually finds all kinds
of lofty reasons for siding with the strong against the
weak. A Luther, who, when first defying the established
church, spoke feelingly of "the poor, simple, common
folk,"[7] proclaimed later, when allied with the German
princelings, that "God would prefer to suffer the government to exist no matter how evil, rather than to allow the
rabble to riot, no matter how justified they are in doing
so."[8] A Burke patronized by lords and nobles spoke of the
"swinish multitude" and recommended to the poor "patience, labor, sobriety, frugality, and religion."[9] The pam-
pered and flattered men of words in Nazi Germany and
Bolshevik Russia feel no impulsion to side with the per-
secuted and terrorized against the ruthless leaders and
their secret police.

106

Whenever we find a dispensation enduring beyond its
span of competence, there is either an entire absence of
an educated class or an intimate alliance between those
in power and the men of words. Where all learned men are
clergymen, the church is unassailable. Where all learned
men are bureaucrats or where education gives a man an
acknowledged superior status, the prevailing order is
likely to be free from movements of protest.

The Catholic Church sank to its lowest level in the tenth
century, at the time of Pope John XII. It was then far more
corrupt and ineffectual than at the time of the Reformation. But in the tenth century all learned men were priests,

whereas in the fifteenth century, as the result of the introduction of printing and paper, learning had ceased to be the monopoly of the church. It was the nonclerical humanists who formed the vanguard of the Reformation. Those of the scholars affiliated with the church or who, as in Italy, enjoyed the patronage of the Popes, "showed a tolerant spirit on the whole toward existing institutions, including the ecclesiastical abuses, and, in general, cared little how long the vulgar herd was left in superstitious darkness which befitted their state."[10]

The stability of Imperial China, like that of ancient Egypt, was due to an intimate alliance between the bureaucracy and the literati. It is of interest that the Taiping rebellion, the only effective Chinese mass movement while the Empire was still a going concern, was started by a scholar who failed again and again in the state examination for the highest mandarin caste.[11]

The long endurance of the Roman Empire was due in some degree to the wholehearted partnership between the Roman rulers and the Greek men of words. The conquered Greeks felt that they gave laws and civilization to the conquerors. It is disconcerting to read how the deformed and depraved Nero, who was extravagant in his admiration of Hellas, was welcomed hysterically by the Greeks on his visit in 67 A.D. They took him to their hearts as a fellow intellectual and artist. "To gratify him, all the games had been crowded into a single year. All the cities sent him the prizes of their contests. Committees were continually waiting on him, to beg him to go and sing at every place."[12] And he in turn loaded them with privileges and proclaimed the freedom of Greece at the Isthmian games.

In *A Study of History*, Professor A. J. Toynbee quotes the Latin hexameters which Claudian of Alexandria wrote in praise of Rome almost five hundred years after Caesar set foot on Egyptian soil, and he adds ruefully: "It would be easy to prove that the British Raj had been in many respects a more benevolent and also perhaps a more beneficent institution than the Roman Empire, but it would be hard to find a Claudian in any of the Alexandrias of Hindustan."[13] Now it is not altogether farfetched to assume that, had the British in India instead of cultivating the Nizams, Maharajas, Nawabs, Gekawars and so on made an effort to win the Indian intellectual; had they treated him as an equal, encouraged him in his work and allowed him a share of the fleshpots, they could perhaps have maintained their rule there indefinitely. As it was, the British who ruled India were of a type altogether lacking in the aptitude for getting along with intellectuals in any land, and least of all in India. They were men of action imbued with a faith in the innate superiority of the British. For the most part they scorned the Indian intellectual both as a man of words and as an Indian. The British in India tried to preserve the realm of action for themselves. They did not to any real extent encourage the Indians to become engineers, agronomists or technicians. The educational institutions they established produced "impractical" men of words; and it is an irony of fate that this system, instead of safeguarding British rule, hastened its end.

Britain's failure in Palestine was also due in part to the lack of rapport between the typical British colonial official and men of words. The majority of the Palestinian Jews, although steeped in action, are by upbringing and tradition men of words, and thin-skinned to a fault. They smarted under the contemptuous attitude of the British official who looked on the Jews as on a pack of unmanly and ungrateful quibblers—an easy prey for the warlike Arabs once Britain withdrew its protective hand. The Palestinian Jews also resented the tutelage of mediocre officials, their inferiors in both experience and intelligence. Britons of the caliber of Julian Huxley, Harold Nicolson or Richard Crossman just possibly might have saved Palestine for the Empire.

In both the Bolshevik and the Nazi regimes there is evident an acute awareness of the fateful relation between men of words and the state. In Russia, men of letters, artists and scholars share the privileges of the ruling group. They are all superior civil servants. And though made to toe the party line, they are but subject to the same discipline imposed on the rest of the elite. In the case of Hitler there was a diabolical realism in his plan to make all learning the monopoly of the elite which was to rule his envisioned world empire and keep the anonymous masses barely literate.

107

The men of letters of eighteenth-century France are the most familiar example of intellectuals pioneering a mass movement. A somewhat similar pattern may be detected in the periods preceding the rise of most movements. The ground for the Reformation was prepared by the men who satirized and denounced the clergy in popular pamphlets, and by men of letters like Johann Reuchlin, who fought and discredited the Roman curia. The rapid spread of Christianity in the Roman world was partly due to the fact that the pagan cults it sought to supplant were already thoroughly discredited. The discrediting was done, before and after the birth of Christianity, by the Greek philosophers who were bored with the puerility of the cults and denounced and ridiculed them in schools and city streets. Christianity made little headway against Judaism because the Jewish religion had the ardent allegiance of the Jewish men of words. The rabbis and their disciples enjoyed an exalted status in Jewish life of that day, where the school and the book supplanted the temple and the fatherland. In any social order where the reign of men of words is so supreme, no opposition can develop within and no foreign mass movement can gain a foothold.

The mass movements of modern time, whether socialist or nationalist, were invariably pioneered by poets, writers, historians, scholars, philosophers and the like. The connection between intellectual theoreticians and revolutionary movements needs no emphasis. But it is equally true that all nationalist movements—from the cult of *la patrie* in revolutionary France to the latest nationalist rising in Indonesia—were conceived not by men of action but by faultfinding intellectuals. The generals, industrialists, landowners and businessmen who are considered pillars of patriotism are latecomers who join the movement after it has become a going concern. The most strenuous effort of the early phase of every nationalist movement consists in convincing and winning over these future pillars of patriotism. The Czech historian Palacky said that if the ceiling of a room in which he and a handful of friends were dining one night had collapsed, there would have been no Czech nationalist movement.[14] Such handfuls of impractical men of words were at the beginning of all nationalist movements. German intellectuals were the originators of German nationalism, just as Jewish intellectuals were the originators of Zionism. It is the deep-seated craving of the man of words for an exalted status which makes him oversensitive to any humiliation imposed on the class or community (racial, lingual or religious) to which he belongs however loosely. It was Napoleon's humiliation of the Germans, particularly the Prussians, which drove Fichte and the German intellectuals to call on the German masses to unite into a mighty nation which would dominate Europe. Theodore Herzl and the Jewish intellectuals were driven to Zionism by the humiliations

heaped upon millions of Jews in Russia, and by the calum-
nies to which the Jews in the rest of continental Europe
were subjected toward the end of the nineteenth century.
To a degree the nationalist movement which forced the
British rulers out of India had its inception in the humiliation of a scrawny and bespectacled Indian man of words
in South Africa.

108

It is easy to see how the faultfinding man of words, by
persistent ridicule and denunciation, shakes prevailing
beliefs and loyalties, and familiarizes the masses with the
idea of change. What is not so obvious is the process by
which the discrediting of existing beliefs and institutions
makes possible the rise of a new fanatical faith. For it is
a remarkable fact that the militant man of words who
"sounds the established order to its source to mark its
want of authority and justice"[15] often prepares the ground
not for a society of freethinking individuals but for a corporate society that cherishes utmost unity and blind faith.
A wide diffusion of doubt and irreverence thus leads often
to unexpected results. The irreverence of the Renaissance
was a prelude to the new fanaticism of Reformation and
Counter Reformation. The Frenchmen of the enlightenment who debunked the church and the crown and
preached reason and tolerance released a burst of revolutionary and nationalist fanaticism which has not abated
yet. Marx and his followers discredited religion, nationalism and the passionate pursuit of business, and brought
into being the new fanaticism of socialism, communism,
Stalinist nationalism and the passion for world dominion.
   When we debunk a fanatical faith or prejudice, we do
not strike at the root of fanaticism. We merely prevent its
leaking out at a certain point, with the likely result that it

will leak out at some other point. Thus by denigrating prevailing beliefs and loyalties, the militant man of words unwittingly creates in the disillusioned masses a hunger for faith. For the majority of people cannot endure the barrenness and futility of their lives unless they have some ardent dedication, or some passionate pursuit in which they can lose themselves. Thus, in spite of himself, the scoffing man of words becomes the precursor of a new faith.

The genuine man of words himself can get along without faith in absolutes. He values the search for truth as much as truth itself. He delights in the clash of thought and in the give-and-take of controversy. If he formulates a philosophy and a doctrine, they are more an exhibition of brilliance and an exercise in dialectics than a program of action and the tenets of a faith. His vanity, it is true, often prompts him to defend his speculations with savagery and even venom; but his appeal is usually to reason and not to faith. The fanatics and the faith-hungry masses, however, are likely to invest such speculations with the certitude of holy writ, and make them the fountainhead of a new faith. Jesus was not a Christian, nor was Marx a Marxist.

To sum up, the militant man of words prepares the ground for the rise of a mass movement: 1) by discrediting prevailing creeds and institutions and detaching from them the allegiance of the people; 2) by indirectly creating a hunger for faith in the hearts of those who cannot live without it, so that when the new faith is preached it finds an eager response among the disillusioned masses; 3) by furnishing the doctrine and the slogans of the new faith; 4) by undermining the convictions of the "better people"— those who can get along without faith—so that when the new fanaticism makes its appearance they are without the capacity to resist it. They see no sense in dying for convictions and principles, and yield to the new order without a fight.[16]

Thus when the irreverent intellectual has done his work:

> The best lack all conviction, while the worst
> Are full of passionate intensity.
> Surely some revelation is at hand,
> Surely the Second Coming is at hand.[17]

The stage is now set for the fanatics.

109

The tragic figures in the history of a mass movement are often the intellectual precursors who live long enough to see the downfall of the old order by the action of the masses.

The impression that mass movements, and revolutions in particular, are born of the resolve of the masses to overthrow a corrupt and oppressive tyranny and win for themselves freedom of action, speech and conscience has its origin in the din of words let loose by the intellectual originators of the movement in their skirmishes with the prevailing order. The fact that mass movements as they arise often manifest less individual freedom[18] than the order they supplant, is usually ascribed to the trickery of a power-hungry clique that kidnaps the movement at a critical stage and cheats the masses of the freedom about to dawn. Actually, the only people cheated in the process are the intellectual precursors. They rise against the established order, deride its irrationality and incompetence, denounce its illegitimacy and oppressiveness, and call for freedom of self-expression and self-realization. They take it for granted that the masses who respond to their call and range themselves behind them crave the same things. However, the freedom the masses crave is not freedom of self-expression and self-realization, but freedom from the intolerable burden of an autonomous existence. They want freedom from "the fearful burden of free choice,"[19] freedom from the arduous responsibility of realizing their ineffectual selves and shouldering the blame for the blemished product. They do not want freedom of conscience, but faith—blind, authoritarian faith. They sweep away the old order not to create a society of free and independent men, but to establish uniformity, individual anonymity and a new structure of perfect unity. It is not the wickedness of the old regime they rise against but its weakness; not its oppression, but its failure to hammer them together into one solid, mighty whole. The persuasiveness of the intellectual demagogue consists not so much in convicting people of the vileness of the established order as in demonstrating its helpless incompetence. The immediate result of a mass movement usually corresponds to what the people want. They are not cheated in the process.

The reason for the tragic fate which almost always overtakes the intellectual midwives of a mass movement is that, no matter how much they preach and glorify the united effort, they remain essentially individualists. They believe in the possibility of individual happiness and the validity of individual opinion and initiative. But once a movement gets rolling, power falls into the hands of those who have neither faith in, nor respect for, the individual. And the reason they prevail is not so much that their disregard of the individual gives them a capacity for ruthlessness, but that their attitude is in full accord with the ruling passion of the masses.

XVI

The Fanatics

110

When the moment is ripe, only the fanatic can hatch a genuine mass movement. Without him the disaffection engendered by militant men of words remains undirected and can vent itself only in pointless and easily suppressed disorders. Without him the initiated reforms, even when drastic, leave the old way of life unchanged, and any change in government usually amounts to no more than a transfer of power from one set of men of action to another. Without him there can perhaps be no new beginning.

When the old order begins to fall apart, many of the vociferous men of words, who prayed so long for the day, are in a funk. The first glimpse of the face of anarchy frightens them out of their wits. They forget all they said about the "poor simple folk" and run for help to strong men of action—princes, generals, administrators, bankers, landowners—who know how to deal with the rabble and how to stem the tide of chaos.

Not so the fanatic. Chaos is his element. When the old order begins to crack, he wades in with all his might and recklessness to blow the whole hated present to high heaven. He glories in the sight of a world coming to a sudden end. To hell with reforms! All that already exists is rubbish, and there is no sense in reforming rubbish. He justifies his will to anarchy with the plausible assertion that there can be no new beginning so long as the old clutters the landscape. He shoves aside the frightened men of words, if they are still around, though he continues to extol their doctrines and mouth their slogans. He alone knows the innermost craving of the masses in action: the craving for communion, for the mustering of the host, for the dissolution of cursed individuality in the majesty and grandeur of a mighty whole. Posterity is king; and woe to those, inside and outside the movement, who hug and hang on to the present.

111

Whence come the fanatics? Mostly from the ranks of the noncreative men of words. The most significant division between men of words is between those who can find fulfillment in creative work and those who cannot. The creative man of words, no matter how bitterly he may criticize and deride the existing order, is actually attached to the present. His passion is to reform and not to destroy. When the mass movement remains wholly in his keeping, he turns it into a mild affair. The reforms he initiates are of the surface, and life flows on without a sudden break. But such a development is possible only when the anarchic action of the masses does not come into play, either because the old order abdicates without a struggle or because the man of words allies himself with strong men of action the moment chaos threatens to break loose. When the struggle with the old order is bitter and chaotic and victory can be won only by utmost unity and self-sacrifice, the creative man of words is usually shoved aside and the management of affairs falls into the hands of the noncreative men of words—the eternal misfits and the fanatical contemners of the present.[1]

The man who wants to write a great book, paint a great picture, create an architectural masterpiece, become a great scientist, and knows that never in all eternity will he be able to realize this, his innermost desire, can find no peace in a stable social order—old or new. He sees his life as irrevocably spoiled and the world perpetually out of joint. He feels at home only in a state of chaos. Even when he submits to or imposes an iron discipline, he is but submitting to or shaping the indispensable instrument for attaining a state of eternal flux, eternal becoming. Only when engaged in change does he have a sense of freedom and the feeling that he is growing and developing. It is because he can never be reconciled with his self that he fears finality and a fixed order of things. Marat, Robespierre, Lenin, Mussolini and Hitler are outstanding examples of fanatics arising from the ranks of noncreative men of words. Peter Viereck points out that most of the Nazi bigwigs had artistic and literary ambitions which they could not realize. Hitler tried painting and architecture; Goebbels, drama, the novel and poetry; Rosenberg, architecture and philosophy; von Schirach, poetry; Funk, music; Streicher, painting. "Almost all were failures, not only by the usual vulgar criterion of success but by their own artistic criteria." Their artistic and literary ambitions "were originally far deeper than political ambitions: and were integral parts of their personalities."[2]

The creative man of words is ill at ease in the atmosphere of an active movement. He feels that its whirl and passion sap his creative energies. So long as he is conscious of the creative flow within him, he will not find fulfillment in leading millions and in winning victories. The result is that, once the movement starts rolling, he either retires voluntarily or is pushed aside. Moreover, since the genuine man of words can never wholeheartedly and for long suppress his critical faculty, he is inevitably cast in the role of the heretic. Thus unless the creative man of words stifles the newborn movement by allying himself with practical men of action or unless he dies at the right moment, he is likely to end up either a shunned recluse or in exile or facing a firing squad.

112

The danger of the fanatic to the development of a movement is that he cannot settle down. Once victory has been won and the new order begins to crystallize, the fanatic becomes an element of strain and disruption. The taste for strong feeling drives him on to search for mysteries yet to be revealed and secret doors yet to be opened. He keeps groping for extremes. Thus on the morrow of victory most mass movements find themselves in the grip of dissension. The ardor which yesterday found an outlet in a life-and-death struggle with external enemies now vents itself in violent disputes and clash of factions. Hatred has become a habit. With no more outside enemies to destroy, the fanatics make enemies of one another. Hitler—himself a fanatic—could diagnose with precision the state of mind of the fanatics who plotted against him within the ranks of the National Socialist party. In his order to the newly appointed chief of the SA after the purge of Röhm in 1934 he speaks of those who will not settle down: ". . . without realizing it, [they] have found in nihilism their ultimate confession of faith . . . their unrest and disquietude can find satisfaction only in some conspiratorial activity of the mind, in perpetually plotting the disintegration of whatever the set-up of the moment happens to be."[3] As was often the case with Hitler, his accusations against antagonists (inside and outside the Reich) were a self-revelation. He, too, particularly in his last days, found in nihilism his "ultimate philosophy and valediction."[4]

If allowed to have their way, the fanatics may split a movement into schism and heresies which threaten its existence. Even when the fanatics do not breed dissension, they can still wreck the movement by driving it to attempt the impossible. Only the entrance of a practical man of action can save the achievements of the movement.

XVII

The Practical Men of Action

113

A movement is pioneered by men of words, materialized by fanatics and consolidated by men of action.

It is usually an advantage to a movement, and perhaps a prerequisite for its endurance, that these roles should be played by different men succeeding each other as conditions require. When the same person or persons (or the same type of person) leads a movement from its inception to maturity, it usually ends in disaster. The Fascist and Nazi movements were without a successive change in leadership, and both ended in disaster. It was Hitler's fanaticism, his inability to settle down and play the role of a practical man of action, which brought ruin to his movement. Had Hitler died in the middle 1930's, there is little doubt that a man of action of the type of Goering would have succeeded to the leadership and the movement would have survived.

There is of course the possibility of a change in character. A man of words might change into a genuine fanatic or into a practical man of action. Yet the evidence points that such metamorphoses are usually temporary, and that sooner or later there is a reversion to the original type. Trotsky was essentially a man of words—vain, brilliant and an individualist to the core. The cataclysmic collapse of an Empire and Lenin's overpowering will brought him into the camp of the fanatics. In the civil war he displayed unequaled talents as an organizer and general. But the moment the strain relaxed at the end of the civil war, he was a man of words again, without ruthlessness and dark suspicions, putting his trust in words rather than in relentless force, and allowed himself to be pushed aside by the crafty fanatic Stalin.

Stalin himself was a combination of fanatic and man of action, with the fanatical tinge predominating. His disastrous blunders—the senseless liquidation of the kulaks and their offspring, the terror of the purges, the pact with Hitler, the clumsy meddling with the creative work of writers, artists and scientists—were the blunders of a fanatic. There was small chance for the Russians to taste the joys of the present while Stalin, the fanatic, was in power.

Hitler, too, was primarily a fanatic, and his fanaticism vitiated his remarkable achievements as a man of action.

There are, of course, rare leaders such as Lincoln, Gandhi, even F.D.R., Churchill and Nehru. They do not hesitate to harness man's hungers and fears to weld a following and make it zealous unto death in the service of a holy cause; but unlike a Hitler, a Stalin, or even a Luther and a Calvin,[1] they are not tempted to use the slime of frustrated souls as mortar in the building of a new world. The self-confidence of these rare leaders is derived from and blended with their faith in humanity, for they know that no one can be honorable unless he honors mankind.

114

The man of action saves the movement from the suicidal dissensions and the recklessness of the fanatics. But his appearance usually marks the end of the dynamic phase of the movement. The war with the present is over. The genuine man of action is intent not on renovating the world but on possessing it. Whereas the life breath of the dynamic phase was protest and a desire for drastic change, the final phase is chiefly preoccupied with administering and perpetuating the power won.

With the appearance of the man of action the explosive vigor of the movement is embalmed and sealed in sanctified institutions. A religious movement crystallizes in a hierarchy and a ritual; a revolutionary movement, in organs of vigilance and administration; a nationalist movement, in governmental and patriotic institutions. The establishment of a church marks the end of the revivalist spirit; the organs of a triumphant revolution liquidate the revolutionary mentality and technique; the governmental institutions of a new or revived nation put an end to chauvinistic belligerence. The institutions freeze a pattern of united action. The members of the institutionalized collective body are expected to act as one man, yet they must represent a loose aggregation rather than a spontaneous coalescence. They must be unified only through their unquestioning loyalty to the institutions. Spontaneity is suspect, and duty is prized above devotion.

115

The chief preoccupation of a man of action when he takes over an "arrived" movement is to fix and perpetuate its unity and readiness for self-sacrifice. His ideal is a compact, invincible whole that functions automatically. To achieve this he cannot rely on enthusiasm, for enthusiasm is ephemeral. Persuasion, too, is unpredictable. He inclines, therefore, to rely mainly on drill and coercion. He finds the assertion that all men are cowards less debatable than that all men are fools, and, in the words of Sir John Maynard, inclines to found the new order on the necks of the people rather than in their hearts.[2] The genuine man of action is not a man of faith but a man of law.

Still, he cannot help being awed by the tremendous achievements of faith and spontaneity in the early days of the movement when a mighty instrument of power was conjured out of the void. The memory of it is still extremely vivid. He takes, therefore, great care to preserve in the new institutions an impressive façade of faith, and maintains an incessant flow of fervent propaganda, though he relies mainly on the persuasiveness of force. His orders are worded in pious vocabulary, and the old formulas and slogans are continually on his lips. The symbols of faith are carried high and given reverence. The men of words and the fanatics of the early period are canonized. Though the steel fingers of coercion make themselves felt everywhere and great emphasis is placed on mechanical drill, the pious phrases and the fervent propaganda give to coercion a semblance of persuasion, and to habit a semblance of spontaneity. No effort is spared to present the new order as the glorious consummation of the hopes and struggles of the early days.

The man of action is eclectic in the methods he uses to endow the new order with stability and permanence. He borrows from near and far and from friend and foe. He even goes back to the old order which preceded the movement and appropriates from it many techniques of stability, thus unintentionally establishing continuity with the past. The institution of an absolute dictator which is characteristic of this stage is as much the deliberate employment of a device as the manifestation of a sheer hunger for power. Byzantinism is likely to be conspicuous both at the birth and the decline of an organization. It is the expression of a desire for a stable pattern, and it can be used either to give shape to the as yet amorphous, or to hold together that which seems to be falling apart. The infallibility of the bishop of Rome was propounded by Irenaeus (second century) in the earliest days of the papacy, and by Pius IX in 1870, when the papacy seemed to be on the brink of extinction.

Thus the order evolved by a man of action is a patchwork. Stalin's Russia was a patchwork of bolshevism, czarism, nationalism, pan-Slavism, dictatorship and borrowings from Hitler, and monopolistic capitalism. Hitler's Third Reich was a conglomerate of nationalism, racialism, Prussianism, dictatorship and borrowings from fascism, bolshevism, Shintoism, Catholicism and the ancient Hebrews. Christianity, too, when after the conflicts and dissensions of the first few centuries it crystallized into an authoritarian church, was a patchwork of old and new and of borrowings from friend and foe. It patterned its hierarchy after the bureaucracy of the Roman Empire, adopted portions of the antique ritual, developed the institution of an absolute leader and used every means to absorb all existent elements of life and power.[3]

116

In the hands of a man of action the mass movement ceases to be a refuge from the agonies and burdens of an individual existence and becomes a means of self-realization for the ambitious. The irresistible attraction which the movement now exerts on those preoccupied with their individual careers is a clear-cut indication of the drastic change in its character and of its reconciliation with the present. It is also clear that the influx of these career men accelerates the transformation of the movement into an enterprise. Hitler, who had a clear vision of the whole course of a movement even while he was nursing his infant National Socialism, warned that a movement retains its vigor only so long as it can offer nothing in the present—only "honor and fame in the eyes of posterity," and that when it is invaded by those who want to make the most of the present "the 'mission' of such a movement is done for."[4]

The movement at this stage still concerns itself with the frustrated—not to harness their discontent in a deadly struggle with the present, but to reconcile them with it; to make them patient and meek. To them it offers the distant hope, the dream and the vision.[5] Thus at the end of its vigorous span the movement is an instrument of power for the successful and an opiate for the frustrated.

XVIII

Good and Bad Mass Movements

THE UNATTRACTIVENESS AND STERILITY OF THE ACTIVE PHASE

117

This book concerns itself chiefly with the active phase of mass movements—the phase molded and dominated by the true believer. It is in this phase that mass movements of all types often manifest the common traits we have tried to outline. Now it seems to be true that no matter how noble the original purpose of a movement and however beneficent the end result, its active phase is bound to strike us as unpleasant if not evil. The fanatic who personifies this phase is usually an unattractive human type. He is ruthless, self-righteous, credulous, disputatious, petty and rude. He is often ready to sacrifice relatives and friends for his holy cause. The absolute unity and the readiness for self-sacrifice which give an active movement its irresistible drive and enable it to undertake the impossible are usually achieved at a sacrifice of much that is pleasant and precious in the autonomous individual. No mass movement, however sublime its faith and worthy its purpose, can be good if its active phase is overlong, and, particularly, if it is continued after the movement is in undisputed possession of power. Such mass movements as we consider more or less beneficent—the Reformation, the Puritan, French and American Revolutions, and many

of the nationalist movements of the past hundred years—
had active phases which were relatively short, though
while they lasted they bore, to a greater or lesser degree,
the imprint of the fanatic. The mass movement leader who
benefits his people and humanity knows not only how to
start a movement, but, like Gandhi, when to end its active
phase.

Where a mass movement preserves for generations the
pattern shaped by its active phase (as in the case of the
militant church through the Middle Ages), or where by a
successive accession of fanatical proselytes its orthodoxy
is continually strengthened (as in the case of Islam[1]), the
result is an era of stagnation—a dark age. Whenever we
find a period of genuine creativeness associated with a
mass movement, it is almost always a period which either
precedes or, more often, follows the active phase. Pro-
vided the active phase of the movement is not too long and
does not involve excessive bloodletting and destruction,
its termination, particularly when it is abrupt, often re-
leases a burst of creativeness. This seems to be true both
when the movement ends in triumph (as in the case of the
Dutch Rebellion) or when it ends in defeat (as in the case
of the Puritan Revolution). It is not the idealism and the
fervor of the movement which are the cause of any cultural renascence which may follow it, but rather the
abrupt relaxation of collective discipline and the liberation of the individual from the stifling atmosphere of blind
faith and the disdain of his self and the present. Sometimes the craving to fill the void left by the lost or deserted
holy cause becomes a creative impulse.[2]

The active phase itself is sterile. Trotsky knew that
"Periods of high tension in social passions leave little
room for contemplation and reflection. All the muses—
even the plebeian muse of journalism in spite of her sturdy
hips—have hard sledding in times of revolution."[3] On the

other hand, Napoleon[4] and Hitler were mortified by the anemic quality of the literature and art produced in their heroic age and clamored for masterpieces which would be worthy of the mighty deeds of the times. They had not an inkling that the atmosphere of an active movement cripples or stifles the creative spirit. Milton, who in 1640 was a poet of great promise, with a draft of *Paradise Lost* in his pocket, spent twenty sterile years of pamphlet writing while he was up to his neck in the "sea of noises and hoarse disputes"[5] which was the Puritan Revolution. With the Revolution dead and himself in disgrace, he produced *Paradise Lost, Paradise Regained* and *Samson Agonistes.*

118

The interference of an active mass movement with the creative process is deep-reaching and manifold: 1) The fervor it generates drains the energies which would have flowed into creative work. Fervor has the same effect on creativeness as dissipation. 2) It subordinates creative work to the advancement of the movement. Literature, art and science must be propagandistic and they must be "practical." The true-believing writer, artist or scientist does not create to express himself, or to save his soul or to discover the true and the beautiful. His task, as he sees it, is to warn, to advise, to urge, to glorify and to denounce. 3) Where a mass movement opens vast fields of action (war, colonization, industrialization), there is an additional drain of creative energy. 4) The fanatical state of mind by itself can stifle all forms of creative work. The fanatic's disdain for the present blinds him to the complexity and uniqueness of life. The things which stir the creative worker seem to him either trivial or corrupt. "Our writers must march in serried ranks, and he who steps off the road to pick flowers is like a deserter." These words of Konstantine Simonov echo the thought and the very words of fanatics through the ages. Said Rabbi Jacob (first century, A.D.): "He who walks in the way ... and interrupts his study [of the Torah] saying: 'How beautiful is this tree' [or] 'How beautiful is this ploughed field' ... [has] made himself guilty against his own soul."[6] St. Bernard of Clerveaux could walk all day by the lake of Geneva and never see the lake. In *Refinement of the Arts* David Hume tells of the monk "who, because the windows of his cell opened upon a noble prospect, made a covenant with his eyes never to turn that way." The blindness of the fanatic is a source of strength (he sees no obstacles), but it is the cause of intellectual sterility and emotional monotony.

The fanatic is also mentally cocky, and hence barren of new beginnings. At the root of his cockiness is the conviction that life and the universe conform to a simple formula—his formula. He is thus without the fruitful intervals of groping, when the mind is as it were in solution—ready for all manner of new reactions, new combinations and new beginnings.

119

When an active mass movement displays originality, it is usually an originality of application and of scale. The principles, methods, techniques, etcetera which a mass movement applies and exploits are usually the product of a creativeness which was or still is active outside the sphere of the movement. All active mass movements have that unabashed imitativeness which we have come to associate with the Japanese. Even in the field of propaganda the Nazis and the Communists imitate more than they originate. They sell their brand of holy cause the way the capitalist advertiser sells his brand of soap or cigarettes.[7] Much that strikes us as new in the methods of the Nazis

and Communists stems from the fact that they are running
(or trying to run) vast territorial empires the way a Ford
or a DuPont runs his industrial empire. It is perhaps true
that the success of the Communist experiment will always
depend on the unfettered creativeness proceeding in the
outside non-Communist world. The brazen men in the
Kremlin think it a magnanimous concession when they
say that communism and capitalism can continue for long
side by side. Actually, if there were no free societies outside the Communist orbit, they might have found it necessary to establish them by ukase.

SOME FACTORS WHICH DETERMINE THE LENGTH OF THE ACTIVE PHASE

120

A mass movement with a concrete, limited objective is
likely to have a shorter active phase than a movement
with a nebulous, indefinite objective. The vague objective
is perhaps indispensable for the development of chronic
extremism. Said Oliver Cromwell: "A man never goes so
far as when he does not know whither he is going."[8]

When a mass movement is set in motion to free a nation
from tyranny, either domestic or foreign, or to resist an
aggressor, or to renovate a backward society, there is a
natural point of termination once the struggle with the
enemy is over or the process of reorganization is nearing
completion. On the other hand, when the objective is an
ideal society of perfect unity and selflessness—whether it
be the City of God, a Communist heaven on earth, or
Hitler's warrior state—the active phase is without an automatic end. Where unity and self-sacrifice are indispensable for the normal functioning of a society, everyday life
is likely to be either religiofied (common tasks turned into

holy causes) or militarized. In either case, the pattern developed by the active phase is likely to be fixed and perpetuated. Jacob Burckhardt and Ernest Renan were among the very few in the hopeful second half of the nineteenth century who sensed the ominous implications lurking in the coming millennium. Burckhardt saw the militarized society: "I have a premonition which sounds like utter folly, and yet which positively will not leave me: the military state must become one great factory. . . . What must logically come is a definite and supervised stint of misery, with promotions and in uniform, daily begun and ended to the sound of drums."[9] Renan's insight went deeper. He felt that socialism was the coming religion of the Occident, and that being a secular religion it would lead to a religi-ofication of politics and economics. He also feared a revival of Catholicism as a reaction against the new religion: "Let us tremble. At this very moment, perchance, the religion of the future is in the making; and we have no part in it! . . . Credulity has deep roots. Socialism may bring back by the complicity of Catholicism a new Middle Age, with barbarians, churches, eclipses of liberty and individuality—in a word, of civilization."[10]

121

There is perhaps some hope to be derived from the fact that in most instances where an attempt to realize an ideal society gave birth to the ugliness and violence of a prolonged active mass movement the experiment was made on a vast scale and with a heterogeneous population. Such was the case in the rise of Christianity and Islam, and in the French, Russian and Nazi revolutions. The promising communal settlements in the small state of Israel and the successful programs of socialization in the small Scandinavian states indicate perhaps that when the attempt to realize an ideal society is undertaken by a small nation with a more or less homogeneous population it can proceed and succeed in an atmosphere which is neither hectic nor coercive. The horror a small nation has of wasting its precious human material, its urgent need for internal harmony and cohesion as a safeguard against aggression from without, and, finally, the feeling of its people that they are all of one family make it possible to foster a readiness for utmost co-operation without recourse to either religiofication or militarization. It would probably be fortunate for the Occident if the working out of all extreme social experiments were left wholly to small states with homogeneous, civilized populations. The principle of a pilot plant, practiced in the large mass-production industries, could thus perhaps be employed in the realization of social progress. That the small nations should give the Occident the blueprint of a hopeful future would in itself be part of a long established pattern. For the small states of the Middle East, Greece and Italy, have given us our religion and the essential elements of our culture and civilization.

There is one other connection between the quality of the masses and the nature and duration of an active mass movement. The fact is that the Japanese, Russians and Germans, who allow the interminable continuation of an active mass movement without a show of opposition, were inured to submissiveness or iron discipline for generations before the rise of their respective modern mass movements. Lenin was aware of the enormous advantage the submissiveness of the Russian masses gave him: "how can you compare [he exclaimed] the masses of Western Europe with our people—so patient, so accustomed to privation?"[11] Whoever reads what Madame de Staël said of the Germans over a century ago cannot but realize what ideal material they are for an interminable mass movement: "The Germans," she said, "are vigorously submissive. They employ philosophical reasonings to explain what is the least philosophic thing in the world, respect for force and the fear which transforms that respect into admiration."[12]

One cannot maintain with certitude that it would be impossible for a Hitler or a Stalin to rise in a country with an established tradition of freedom. What can be asserted with some plausibility is that in a traditionally free country a Hitler or a Stalin might not find it too difficult to gain power but extremely hard to maintain himself indefinitely. Any marked improvement in economic conditions would almost certainly activate the tradition of freedom which is a tradition of revolt. In Russia, as pointed out in Section 45, the individual who pitted himself against Stalin had nothing to identify himself with, and his capacity to resist coercion was nil. But in a traditionally free country the individual who pits himself against coercion does not feel an isolated human atom but one of a mighty race—his rebellious ancestors.

122

The personality of the leader is probably a crucial factor in determining the nature and duration of a mass movement. Such rare leaders as Lincoln and Gandhi not only try to curb the evil inherent in a mass movement but are willing to put an end to the movement when its objective is more or less realized. They are of the very few in whom "power [has] developed a grandeur and generosity of the soul."[13] Stalin's medieval mind and his tribal ruthlessness were chief factors in the prolonged dynamism of the Communist movement. It is futile to speculate on what the Russian Revolution might have been like had Lenin lived a decade or two longer. One has the impression that he was without that barbarism of the soul so evident in Hitler and Stalin, which, as Heraclitus said, makes our eyes and ears "evil witnesses to the doings of men." Stalin molded his possible successors in his own image, and the Russian people can probably expect more of the same for the next several decades. Cromwell's death brought the end of the Puritan Revolution, while the death of Robespierre marked the end of the active phase of the French Revolution. Had Hitler died in the middle of the 1930's, Nazism would probably have shown, under the leadership of a Goering, a fundamental change in its course, and the Second World War might have been averted. Yet the sepulcher of Hitler, the founder of a Nazi religion, might perhaps have been a greater evil than all the atrocities, bloodshed and destruction of Hitler's war.

123

The manner in which a mass movement starts out can also have some effect on the duration and mode of termination of the active phase of the movement. When we see the Reformation, the Puritan, American and French revolutions and many of the nationalist uprisings terminate, after a relatively short active phase, in a social order marked by increased individual liberty, we are witnessing the realization of moods and examples which characterized the earliest days of these movements. All of them started out by defying and overthrowing a long-established authority. The more clear-cut this initial act of defiance and the more vivid its memory in the minds of the people, the more likely is the eventual emergence of individual liberty. There was no such clear-cut act of defiance in the rise of Christianity. It did not start by overthrowing a king, a hierarchy, a state or a church. Martyrs there were, but not individuals shaking their fists under the nose of proud authority and defying it in the view of the whole world.[14] Hence perhaps the fact that the authoritarian order ushered in by Christianity endured almost unchallenged for fifteen hundred years. The eventual emancipation of the Christian mind at the time of the Renaissance in Italy drew its inspiration not from the history of early Christianity but from the stirring examples of individual independence and defiance in the Graeco-Roman past. There is a similar lack of a dramatic act of defiance at the birth of Islam and of the Japanese collective body, and in neither are there even now signs of genuine individual emancipation. German nationalism, too, unlike the nationalism of most Western countries, did not start with a spectacular act of defiance against established authority. It was taken under the wing from its beginning by the Prussian army.[15] The seed of individual liberty in Germany is in its Protestantism and not its nationalism. The Reformation, the American, French and Russian revolutions and most of the nationalist movements opened with a grandiose overture of individual defiance, and the memory of it is kept green.

By this test, the eventual emergence of individual liberty in Russia is perhaps not entirely hopeless.

USEFUL MASS MOVEMENTS

124

In the eyes of the true believer, people who have no holy cause are without backbone and character—a pushover for men of faith. On the other hand, the true believers of various hues, though they view each other with mortal hatred and are ready to fly at each other's throats, recognize and respect each other's strength. Hitler looked on the Bolsheviks as his equals and gave orders that former Communists should be admitted to the Nazi party at once. Stalin in his turn saw in the Nazis and the Japanese the only nations worthy of respect. Even the religious fanatic and the militant atheist are not without respect for each other. Dostoyevsky puts the following words in Bishop Tihon's mouth: "outright atheism is more to be respected than worldly indifference . . . the complete atheist stands on the penultimate step to most perfect faith, . . . but the indifferent person has no faith whatever except a bad fear."[16]

All the true believers of our time—whether Communist, Nazi, Fascist, Japanese or Catholic—declaimed volubly (and the Communists still do) on the decadence of the Western democracies. The burden of their talk is that in the democracies people are too soft, too pleasure-loving and too selfish to die for a nation, a God or a holy cause. This lack of a readiness to die, we are told, is indicative of an inner rot—a moral and biological decay. The democracies are old, corrupt and decadent. They are no match for the virile congregations of the faithful who are about to inherit the earth.

There is a grain of sense and more than a grain of nonsense in these declamations. The readiness for united action and self-sacrifice is, as indicated in Section 43, a mass movement phenomenon. In normal times a democratic nation is an institutionalized association of more or less free individuals. When its existence is threatened and it has to unify its people and generate in them a spirit of utmost self-sacrifice, the democratic nation must transform itself into something akin to a militant church or a revolutionary party. This process of religiofication, though often difficult and slow, does not involve deep-reaching changes. The true believers themselves imply that the "decadence" they declaim about so volubly is not an organic decay. According to the Nazis, Germany was decadent in the 1920's and wholly virile in the 1930's. Surely a decade is too short a time to work significant biological or even cultural changes in a population of millions.

It is nevertheless true that in times like the Hitler decade the ability to produce a mass movement in short order is of vital importance to a nation. The mastery of the art of religiofication is an essential requirement in the leader of a democratic nation, even though the need to practice it might not arise. And it is perhaps true that extreme intellectual fastidiousness or a businessman's practical-mindedness disqualifies a man for national leadership. There are also perhaps certain qualities in the normal life of a democratic nation which can facilitate the process of religiofication in time of crisis and are therefore the elements of a potential national virility. The measure of a nation's potential virility is as the reservoir of its longing. The saying of Heraclitus that "it would not be better for mankind if they were given their desires" is true of nations as well as of individuals. When a nation ceases to want things fervently or directs its desires toward an ideal that is concrete and limited, its potential virility is impaired. Only a goal which lends itself to continued perfection can keep a nation potentially virile even though its desires are continually fulfilled. The goal need not be sublime. The gross ideal of an ever-rising standard of living has kept this nation fairly virile. England's ideal of the country gentleman and France's ideal of the retired rentier are concrete and limited. This definiteness of their national ideal has perhaps something to do with the lessened drive of the two nations. In America, Russia and Germany the ideal is indefinite and unlimited.

125

As indicated in Section 1, mass movements ar
factor in the awakening and renovation of stagna¹ a
ties. Though it cannot be maintained that mas⁻
ments are the only effective instrument of renasc
seems yet to be true that in large and heterogeneou
bodies such as Russia, India, China, the Arabic wor
even Spain, the process of awakening and renovati
pends on the presence of some widespread fervent e
siasm which perhaps only a mass movement can gen
and maintain. When the process of renovation has t
realized in short order, mass movements may be in
pensable even in small homogeneous societies. The
ability to produce a full-fledged mass movement can be
therefore, a grave handicap to a social body. It has probably been one of China's great misfortunes during the past
hundred years that its mass movements (the Taiping rebellion and the Sun Yat-sen revolution) deteriorated or
were stifled too soon. China was unable to produce a
Stalin, a Gandhi or even an Atatürk, who could keep a
genuine mass movement going long enough for drastic
reforms to take root. Ortega y Gasset is of the opinion that
the inability of a country to produce a genuine mass movement indicates some ethnological defect. He says of his
own Spain that its "ethnological intelligence has always
been an atrophied function and has never had a normal
development."[17]

It is probably better for a country that when its government begins to show signs of chronic incompetence it
should be overthrown by a mighty mass upheaval—even
though such overthrow involves a considerable waste of
life and wealth—than that it should be allowed to fall and
crumble of itself. A genuine popular upheaval is often an

ating, renovating and integrating process. Where
i?ments are allowed to die a lingering death, the re-
; often stagnation and decay—perhaps irremediable
y. And since men of words usually play a crucial role
1e rise of mass movements,[18] it is obvious that the
sence of an educated and articulate minority is proba-
/ indispensable for the continued vigor of a social body.
is necessary, of course, that the men of words should not
e in intimate alliance with the established government.
The long social stagnation of the Orient has many causes,
but there is no doubt that one of the most important is the
fact that for centuries the educated were not only few but
almost always part of the government—either as officials
or priests.

The revolutionary effect of the educational work done
by Western colonizing powers has already been mentioned.[19] One wonders whether India's capacity to produce a Gandhi and a Nehru is due less to rare elements
in Indian culture than to the long presence of the British
Rāj. Foreign influence seems to be a prevailing factor in
the process of social renascence. Jewish and Christian
influences were active in the awakening of Arabia at the
time of Mohammed. In the awakening of Europe from the
stagnation of the Middle Ages we also find foreign influences—Graeco-Roman and Arabic. Western influences
were active in the awakening of Russia, Japan and several
Asiatic countries. The important point is that the foreign
influence does not act in a direct way. It is not the introduction of foreign fashions, manners, speech, ways of
thinking and of doing things which shakes a social body
out of its stagnation. The foreign influence acts mainly by
creating an educated minority where there was none
before or by alienating an existing articulate minority
from the prevailing dispensation; and it is this articulate

minority which accomplishes the work of renascence by setting in motion a mass movement. In other words, the foreign influence is merely the first link in a chain of processes, the last link of which is usually a mass movement; and it is the mass movement which shakes the social body out of its stagnation. In the case of Arabia, the foreign influences alienated the man of words, Mohammed, from the prevailing dispensation in Mecca. Mohammed started a mass movement (Islam) which shook and integrated Arabia for a time. In the time of the Renaissance, the foreign influences (Graeco-Roman and Arabic) facilitated the emergence of men of words who had no connection with the church, and also alienated many traditional men of words from the prevailing Catholic dispensation. The resulting movement of the Reformation shook Europe out of its torpor. In Russia, European influence (including Marxism) detached the allegiance of the intelligentsia from the Romanovs, and the eventual Bolshevik revolution is still at work renovating the vast Muscovite Empire. In Japan, the foreign influence reacted not on men of words but on a rare group of men of action which included Emperor Meiji. These practical men of action had the vision which Peter the Great, also a man of action, lacked; and they succeeded where he failed. They knew that the mere introduction of foreign customs and foreign methods would not stir Japan to life, nor could it drive it to make good in decades the backwardness of centuries. They recognized that the art of religiofication is an indispensable factor in so unprecedented a task. They set in motion one of the most effective mass movements of modern times. The evils of this movement are abundantly illustrated throughout this book. Yet it is doubtful whether any other agency of whatever nature could have brought about the phenomenal feat of renovation which has been accomplished in Japan. In Turkey, too, the foreign influence reacted on a man of action, Atatürk, and the last link in the chain was a mass movement.

J. B. S. Haldane counts fanaticism among the only four really important inventions made between 3000 B.C. and 1400 A.D.[20] It was a Judaic-Christian invention. And it is strange to think that in receiving this malady of the soul the world also received a miraculous instrument for raising societies and nations from the dead—an instrument of resurrection.

Notes

Preface

1. The word "frustrated" is not used in this book as a clinical term. It denotes here people who, for one reason or another, feel that their lives are spoiled or wasted.

PART 1

Chapter I

1. E. H. Carr, *Nationalism and After* (New York: Macmillan Company, 1945), p. 20.
2. See end of Section 104.
3. Henry David Thoreau, *Walden,* Modern Library edition (New York: Random House, 1937), p. 69.
4. Alexis de Tocqueville, *On the State of Society in France Before the Revolution of 1789* (London: John Murray, 1888), pp. 198–199.
5. Genesis 11:4, 6.
6. See Section 58.
7. Karl Polanyi, *The Great Transformation* (New York: Farrar and Rinehart, Inc., 1944), p. 35.
8. *Ibid.,* p. 40.

Chapter II

1. Adolph Hitler, *Mein Kampf* (Boston: Houghton Mifflin Company, 1943), p. 105.
2. Hermann Rauschning, *The Conservative Revolution* (New York: G. P. Putnam's Sons, 1941), p. 189.

3. Thomas Gray, *Letters,* Vol. I, p. 137. Quoted by Gamaliel Bradford, *Bare Souls* (New York: Harper & Brothers, 1924), p. 71.

Chapter III

1. Chaim Weizmann, *Trial and Error* (New York: Harper & Brothers, 1949), p. 13.
2. Hermann Rauschning, *Hitler Speaks* (New York: G. P. Putnam's Sons, 1940), p. 134.
3. Konrad Heiden, *Der Fuehrer* (Boston: Houghton Mifflin Company, 1944), p. 30.
4. Fritz August Voigt, *Unto Caesar* (G. P. Putnam's Sons, 1938), p. 283.
5. Carl L. Becker, *The Heavenly City of the Eighteenth-Century Philosophers* (New Haven: Yale University Press, 1932), p. 155.
6. A. Mathiez, "Les Origins des Cultes Revolutionnaires," p. 31. Quoted by Carlton J. H. Hayes, *Essays on Nationalism* (New York: Macmillan Company, 1926), p. 103.
7. Frantz Funck-Brentano, *Luther* (London: Jonathan Cape, Ltd., 1939), p. 278.
8. H. G. Wells, *The Outline of History* (New York: Macmillan Company, 1922), pp. 482–484.

PART 2

Chapter IV

1. A mild instance of the combined shaping by the best and worst is to be observed in the case of language. The respectable middle section of a nation sticks to the dictionary. Innovations come from the best— statesmen, poets, writers, scientists, specialists—and from the worst— slang makers.

Chapter V

1. Charles A. and Mary R. Beard, *The Rise of American Civilization* (New York: Macmillan Company, 1939), Vol. 1, p. 24.
2. Angelica Balabanoff, *My Life as a Rebel* (New York: Harper & Brothers, 1938), p. 204.
3. Edward A. Ross, *The Changing Chinese* (New York: Century Company, 1911), p. 92.
4. Alexis de Tocqueville, *On the State of Society in France Before the Revolution of 1789* (London: John Murray, 1888), p. 149.
5. *Ibid.,* p. 152.
6. Lyford P. Edwards, *The Natural History of Revolution* (Chicago: University of Chicago Press, 1927), p. 70.
7. The Epistle of Paul the Apostle to the Romans 8:25.

8. See Section 116.

9. I. A. R. Wylie, "The Quest of Our Lives," *Reader's Digest*, May 1948, p. 2.

10. Crane Brinton, *A Decade of Revolution* (New York: Harper & Brothers, 1934), p. 161.

11. Ernest Renan, *The Hibbert Lectures, 1880* (London: Williams and Norgate, 1898), Preface.

12. Epictetus, *Discourses*, Book I, Chap. 2.

13. Arthur J. Hubbard, *The Fate of Empires* (New York: Longmans, Green & Company, 1913), p. 170.

14. Matthew 10:35–37.

15. *Ibid.*, 12:47–49.

16. *Ibid.*, 8:22.

17. *Ibid.*, 10:21.

18. Kenneth Scott Latourette, *The Chinese, their History and Culture* (New York: Macmillan Company, 1946), Vol. I, p. 79.

19. Brooks Adams, *The Law of Civilization and Decay* (New York: Alfred A. Knopf, Inc., 1943), p. 142.

20. Quoted by Nicolas Zernov, *Three Russian Prophets* (Toronto: Macmillan Company, 1944), p. 63.

21. Peter F. Drucker, "The Way to Industrial Peace," *Harper's Magazine*, Nov. 1946, p. 392.

22. Kenneth Scott Latourette, *A History of the Expansion of Christianity* (New York: Harper & Brothers, 1937), Vol. I, p. 164.

23. *Ibid.*, p. 23.

24. *Ibid.*, p. 163.

25. Carlton J. H. Hayes, *A Generation of Materialism* (New York: Harper & Brothers, 1941), p. 254.

26. H. G. Wells, *The Outline of History* (New York: Macmillan Company, 1922), p. 719.

27. Theodore Abel, *Why Hitler Came into Power* (New York: Prentice-Hall, 1938), p. 150.

28. Alexis de Tocqueville, *op. cit.*, p. 152.

29. More about veterans in Section 38 and about the relation between armies and mass movements in Section 64.

Chapter VI

1. See Section 111.

Chapter X

1. Hermann Rauschning, *Hitler Speaks* (New York: G. P. Putnam's Sons, 1940), p. 268.

2. *Ibid.*, p. 258.

3. Miriam Beard, *A History of the Businessman* (New York: Macmillan Company, 1938), p. 462.

Chapter XI

1. ". . . Joy shall be in heaven over one sinner that repenteth, more than over ninety and nine just persons, which need no repentance." Luke 15:7. So also in the Talmud (quoted by Joseph Klausner in *Jesus of Nazareth,* p. 380): "Where the repentant stand, the wholly righteous are not worthy to stand."

2. A letter in *Life,* Dec. 23, 1946, written by R. S. Aldrich.

3. See Section 45 on Russian confessions.

4. Quoted by Brooks Adams, *The Law of Civilization and Decay* (New York: Alfred A. Knopf, Inc., 1943), p. 144.

PART 3

Chapter XII

1. See Section 64 on armies.

2. "Of the North American Indians, those had the intensest feeling of unity who were the most warlike." W. G. Sumner, *War and Other Essays* (New Haven: Yale University Press, 1911), p. 15.

Chapter XIII

1. See more on this subject in Section 90.

2. Christopher Burney, *The Dungeon Democracy* (New York: Duell, Sloan & Pearce, 1946), p. 147. See also on the same subject Odd Nansen, *From Day To Day* (New York: G. P. Putnam's Sons, 1949), p. 335; also Arthur Koestler, *The Yogi and the Commissar* (New York: Macmillan Company, 1945), p. 178.

3. For another view of the subject, see Section 20.

4. Ernest Renan, *History of the People of Israel* (Boston: Little, Brown & Company, 1888–1896), Vol. III, p. 416.

5. John Buchan, *Pilgrim's Way* (Boston: Houghton Mifflin Company, 1940), p. 183.

6. Ecclesiastes 1:10.

7. *Ibid.,* 1:9.

8. *Ibid.,* 9:4, 5, 6.

9. There is an echo of this disconcerting truth in a letter from Norway written at the time of the Nazi invasion: "The trouble with us is that we have been so favored in all ways that many of us have lost the true spirit of self-sacrifice. Life has been so pleasant to a great number of people that they are unwilling to risk it seriously." Quoted by J. D. Barry in the San Francisco *News,* June 22, 1940.

10. I Corinthians 1:28.

11. Job 2:4.

12. Luther, "Table Talk, Number 1687." Quoted by Frantz Funck-Brentano, *Luther* (London: Jonathan Cape, Ltd., 1939), p. 246.

13. Henri L. Bergson, *The Two Sources of Morality and Religion* (New York: Henry Holt & Company, 1935).

14. Pascal, *Pensées*.

15. Thomas a Kempis, *Of The Imitation of Christ* (New York: Macmillan Company, 1937), Chap. III.

16. Pascal, *op. cit.*

17. Konrad Heiden, *Der Fuehrer* (Boston: Houghton Mifflin Company, 1944), p. 758.

18. Pascal, *op. cit.*

19. *History of the Communist Party* (Moscow, 1945), p. 355. Quoted by John Fischer, *Why They Behave Like Russians* (New York: Harper & Brothers, 1947), p. 236.

20. Quoted by Emile Cailliet, *The Clue to Pascal* (Toronto: Macmillan Company, 1944).

21. Quoted by Michael Demiashkevich, *The National Mind* (New York: American Book Company, 1938), p. 353.

22. See examples in Section 14.

23. Fëdor Dostoyevsky, *The Idiot*, Part IV, Chap. 7.

24. Ernest Renan, *op. cit.*, Vol. V., p. 159.

25. Harold Ettlinger, *The Axis on the Air* (Indianapolis: Bobbs-Merrill Company, 1943), p. 39.

26. Homer, *Iliad*.

27. Alexis de Tocqueville, *Recollections* (New York: Macmillan Company, 1896), p. 52.

Chapter XIV

1. Heinrich Heine, *Religion and Philosophy in Germany* (London: Trubner & Company, 1882), p. 89.

2. Hermann Rauschning, *Hitler Speaks* (New York: G. P. Putnam's Sons, 1940), p. 234.

3. Fritz August Voigt, *Unto Caesar* (New York: G. P. Putnam's Sons, 1938), p. 301.

4. Adolph Hitler, *Mein Kampf* (Boston: Houghton Mifflin Company, 1943), p. 118.

5. Quoted by Hermann Rauschning, *Hitler Speaks* (New York: G. P. Putnam's Sons, 1940), p. 234.

6. *Ibid.*, p. 235.

7. See Section 100.

8. Crane Brinton, *The Anatomy of Revolution* (New York: W. W. Norton & Company, Inc., 1938), p. 62.

9. *Ibid.*

10. *Ibid.*

11. When John Huss saw an old woman dragging a fagot to add to his funeral pyre, he said: "O sancta simplicitas!" Quoted by Ernest Renan, *The Apostles* (Boston: Roberts Brothers, 1898), p. 43.

12. Pascal, *Pensées*.

13. Hermann Rauschning, *Hitler Speaks* (New York: G. P. Putnam's Sons, 1940), p. 235.

14. Adolph Hitler, *op. cit.*, p. 351.

15. Pascal, *op. cit.*

16. Luther, "Table Talk, Number 2387 a-b." Quoted in Frantz Funck-Brentano, *Luther* (London: Jonathan Cape, Ltd., 1939), p. 319.

17. See Section 60.

18. Matthew 5.

19. Fëdor Dostoyevsky, *The Possessed*, Part II, Chap. 6.

20. Adolph Hitler, *op. cit.*, p. 171.

21. Ernest Renan, *History of the People of Israel* (Boston: Little, Brown & Company, 1888–1896), Vol. I, p. 130.

22. See Sections 96 and 98.

23. The Italian minister of education in 1926. Quoted by Julien Benda, *The Treason of the Intellectuals* (New York: William Morrow Company, 1928), p. 39.

24. For another view on the subject, see Section 33.

25. Niccolo Machiavelli, *The Prince*, Chap. VI.

26. *The Goebbels Diaries* (Garden City: Doubleday & Company, Inc., 1948), p. 460.

27. *Ibid.*, p. 298.

28. Guglielmo Ferrero, *Principles of Power* (New York: G. P. Putnam's Sons, 1942), p. 100.

29. Ernest Renan, *The Poetry of the Celtic Races* (London: W. Scott, Ltd., 1896), essay on Islamism, p. 97.

30. Kenneth Scott Latourette, *The Unquenchable Light* (New York: Harper & Brothers, 1941), p. 33.

31. Kenneth Scott Latourette, *A History of the Expansion of Christianity* (New York: Harper & Brothers, 1937), Vol. I, p. 164.

32. Charles Reginald Haines, *Islam as a Missionary Religion* (London: Society for Promoting Christian Knowledge, 1889), p. 206.

33. Quoted by Frantz Funck-Brentano, *op. cit.*, p. 260.

34. Guglielmo Ferrero, *The Gamble* (Toronto: Oxford University Press, 1939), p. 297.

35. Crane Brinton, *A Decade of Revolution* (New York: Harper & Brothers, 1934), p. 168.

36. "Dominic," *Encyclopaedia Britannica*.

37. Adolph Hitler, *op. cit.*, p. 171.

38. *Ibid.*, p. 171.

39. See Section 45.

40. Jacob Burckhardt, *Force and Freedom* (New York: Pantheon Books, 1943), p. 129.

41. Francis Bacon, "Of Vicissitude of Things," Bacon's *Essays*,

Everyman's Library edition (New York: E. P. Dutton & Company, 1932), p. 171.

42. John Morley, *Notes on Politics and History* (New York: Macmillan Company, 1914), pp. 69–70.

43. Angelica Balabanoff, *My Life as a Rebel* (New York: Harper & Brothers, 1938), p. 156.

44. Frank Wilson Price, "Sun Yat-sen," *Encyclopaedia of the Social Sciences.*

45. Leo XIII, *Sapientiae Christianae.* According to Luther, "Disobedience is a greater sin than murder, unchastity, theft and dishonesty. . . ." Quoted by Jerome Frank, *Fate and Freedom* (New York: Simon and Schuster, Inc., 1945), p. 281.

46. See Sections 78 and 80.

47. Genesis 11:4.

48. Hermann Rauschning, *The Revolution of Nihilism* (Chicago: Alliance Book Corporation, 1939), p. 48.

49. *Ibid.,* p. 40.

50. Ernest Renan, *Antichrist* (Boston: Roberts Brothers, 1897), p. 381.

51. Montaigne, *Essays,* Modern Library edition (New York: Random House, 1946), p. 374.

52. A young Nazi to I. A. R. Wylie shortly before the Second World War. I. A. R. Wylie, "The Quest of Our Lives," *Reader's Digest,* May, 1948, p. 2.

PART 4

Chapter XV

1. See examples in Section 106.

2. G. E. G. Catlin, *The Story of the Political Philosophers* (New York: McGraw-Hill Book Company, 1939), p. 633.

3. Quoted by Alexis de Tocqueville, *Recollections* (New York: Macmillan Company, 1896), p. 331.

4. Multatuli, *Max Havelaar* (New York: Alfred A. Knopf, Inc., 1927). Introduction by D. H. Lawrence.

5. Bertrand Russell, *Proposed Roads to Freedom* (New York: Blue Ribbon Books, 1931). Introduction, p. viii.

6. Henry Thoreau, *Walden,* Modern Library edition (New York: Random House, 1937), p. 70.

7. In his letter to the Archbishop of Mainz accompanying his theses. Quoted by Frantz Funck-Brentano, *Luther* (London: Jonathan Cape, Ltd., 1939), p. 65.

8. Quoted by Jerome Frank, *Fate and Freedom* (New York: Simon and Schuster, Inc., 1945), p. 281.

9. *Ibid.,* p. 133.

10. "Reformation," *Encyclopaedia Britannica.*

11. René Fülöp Miller, *Leaders, Dreamers and Rebels* (New York: The Viking Press, 1935), p. 85.

12. Ernest Renan, *Antichrist* (Boston: Roberts Brothers, 1897), p. 245.

13. Arnold J. Toynbee, *A Study of History.* Abridgement by D. C. Somervell (Toronto: Oxford University Press, 1947), p. 423.

14. Carlton J. H. Hayes, *The Historical Evolution of Modern Nationalism* (New York: R. R. Smith, 1931), p. 294.

15. Pascal, *Pensées.*

16. Demaree Bess quotes a Dutch banker in Holland in 1941: "We do not want to become martyrs any more than most modern people want martyrdom." "The Bitter Fate of Holland," *Saturday Evening Post,* Feb. 1, 1941.

17. William Butler Yeats, "The Second Coming," *Collected Poems* (New York: Macmillan Company, 1933).

18. See Section 27.

19. Fëdor Dostoyevsky, *The Brothers Karamazov,* Book V, Chap. 5.

Chapter XVI

1. See Section 37.

2. Peter Viereck, *Metapolitics* (New York: Alfred A. Knopf, 1941), pp. 156 and 170.

3. Hans Bernd Gisevius, *To the Bitter End* (Boston: Houghton Mifflin Company, 1947), pp. 121–122.

4. H. R. Trevor-Roper, *The Last Days of Hitler* (New York: Macmillan Company, 1947), p. 4.

Chapter XVII

1. Both Luther and Calvin "aimed to set up a new church authority which would be more powerful, more dictatorial and exacting, and far more diligent in persecuting heretics, than the Catholic Church." Jerome Frank, *Fate and Freedom* (New York: Simon and Schuster, Inc., 1945), p. 283.

2. John Maynard, *Russia in Flux* (London: Victor Gollancz, Ltd., 1941), p. 19.

3. John Addington Symonds, *The Fine Arts* "Renaissance in Italy" series (London: Smith, Elder & Company, 1906), pp. 19–20.

4. Adolph Hitler, *Mein Kampf* (Boston: Houghton Mifflin Company, 1943), p. 105.

5. See Section 25.

Chapter XVIII

1. See Section 85.

2. For example, review the careers of Milton and Bunyan, Koestler and Silone.

3. Leon Trotsky, *The History of the Russian Revolution* (New York: Simon and Schuster, Inc., 1932). Preface.

4. "It was Napoleon who wrote to his Commissioner of Police asking him why there was no flourishing literature in the Empire and please to see to it that there was." Jacques Barzun, *Of Human Freedom* (Boston: Little, Brown & Company, 1939), p. 91.

5. "John Milton," *Encyclopaedia Britannica.*

6. Pirke Aboth, *The Sayings of the Jewish Fathers* (New York: E. P. Dutton & Company, Inc., 1929), p. 36.

7. Eva Lips, *Savage Symphony* (New York: Random House, 1938), p. 18.

8. Quoted by J. A. Cramb, *The Origins and Destiny of Imperial Britain* (London: John Murray, 1915), p. 216.

9. In a letter to his friend Preen. Quoted by James Hastings Nichols in his introduction to the English translation of Jacob C. Burckhardt's *Force and Freedom* (New York: Pantheon Books, 1943), p. 40.

10. Ernest Renan, *History of the People of Israel* (Boston: Little, Brown & Company, 1888–1896), Vol. V, p. 360.

11. Angelica Balabanoff, *My Life as a Rebel* (New York: Harper & Brothers, 1938), p. 281.

12. Quoted by W. R. Inge, "Patriotism," *Nineteen Modern Essays,* ed. W. A. Archbold (New York: Longmans, Green & Company, 1926), p. 213.

13. John Maynard, *Russia in Flux* (London: Victor Gollancz, Ltd., 1941), p. 29.

14. "The Christian resistance to authority was indeed more than heroic, but it was not heroic." Sir J. R. Seeley, *Lectures and Essays* (London: Macmillan, 1895), p. 81.

15. Said Hardenberg to the King of Prussia after the defeat at Jena: "Your Majesty, we must do from above what the French have done from below."

16. Fëdor Dostoyevsky, *The Possessed,* Modern Library edition (New York: Random House, 1936), p. 698.

17. José Ortega y Gasset, *The Modern Theme* (New York: W. W. Norton & Company, 1931), p. 128.

18. See Section 104 and following.

19. See Section 104.

20. J. B. S. Haldane, *The Inequality of Man* (New York: Famous Books, Inc., 1938), p. 49.

Malcolm B. Roberts, Anchorage, Alaska

About the Author

ERIC HOFFER (1902–1983) was self-educated. He worked in restaurants, and as a migrant field-worker and gold prospector. After Pearl Harbor, he worked as a longshoreman in San Francisco for twenty-five years. The author of more than ten books, including *The Passionate State of Mind*, *The Ordeal of Change*, and *The Temper of Our Time*, Eric Hoffer was awarded the Presidential Medal of Freedom in 1983.